A Parent's Guide to
School
Projects

Kathie Weir

parent's
guide
press

los angeles ca

A Parent's Guide™ to
School Projects

This book and all titles in the Parent's Guide series are available to fundraisers, educational institutions, parent or teacher organizations, schools, government agencies and corporations at a discount for purchases of more than 10 units. For larger purchases, Parent's Guides may be customized with corporate or institutional logos, specialized articles or other features. Persons or organizations wishing to inquire should call **Mars Publishing** at **1-800-549-6646** or write to us at **sales@marspub.com**.

parent's guide press

Edwin E. Steussy, CEO and Publisher
Lars W. Peterson, Project Editor
Michael P. Duggan, Graphic Artist

PO Box 461730
Los Angeles CA 90046
www.pgpress.com

contents

contents

contents

author's note

Dedication

This book is dedicated to my late grandmother, Mary Lyanda Dullea, who taught school for fifty years and loved every minute of it, and to my children, Sierra Dullea Weir and Brett Madsen Weir, who continue to amaze and enchant me.

Acknowledgements

Thanks to everyone who helped me write this book, especially the excellent and professional Parent's Guide Press team: Edwin E. Steussy, publisher; Lars W. Peterson, editor; Michael P. Duggan, graphic artist; and Alice Suh, marketing. I give them the pictures and words, but they turn it into a book. Thanks to Rick Laughlin for his magic and to Dave and Earline Weir for their much-appreciated moral support. Thanks to Sierra Weir, photographer extraordinaire, and to Sierra and Brett Weir and all the other students who allowed me to photograph their incredible school projects for this book.

I would like to thank all of the generous (mostly anonymous) teachers who gave me assistance by filling out surveys, as well as those who helped me brainstorm ideas for this book, i.e., Judy Holman, Angie D'Aleo, Kevin Allen, and Linda Velasco. A special thank you goes to the creative and energetic teachers who allowed me to include copies of their favorite projects in Appendix A, photograph their classrooms, and obtain permission to use photos of individual students' projects. From White Point Elementary School in San Pedro, California: Charlotte Murai, Kindergarten; Jeffrey Clay, 3rd Grade; Eunice Morita, 4th Grade; Bruce Dalrymple, 5th Grade; and Rachel Ahumada, Secretary. From Dodson Middle School and Gifted and High Ability Magnet, in RPV, California: Michelle Bethune, 7th Grade English; Laura J.

author's note

Freeman, 6th Grade English and Social Studies; Joyce Kimura, 7th Grade Math; Raymond Moser, 7th Grade Social Studies; Karen Kromer, 6th Grade Math and Science; Linda Velasco, 8th Grade English; Matt Sprenger, 6th Grade Math and Science; Anthony Louros, 6th Grade Math and Science; Teresa L. Baumann, 8th Grade Social Studies; and Alan Kusumoto, 7th Grade Science; Kathy Newman, Assistant Principal; and Claudia Dunn, Magnet Coordinator. Your contributions will help parents and students everywhere.

Your Input Is Needed

As a parent and teacher in Southern California, I have written from my personal experiences and from contributions from teachers in the region. Needs are undoubtedly different in other areas of the country, and I'd love to know about them. If you have something that you'd like to see covered or corrected in the second edition of this book, please let me and my publisher know by sending an email to comments@marspub.com. If your suggestion is included in the next edition, I will send you a free copy the book, as well as credit you for the submission.

Introduction

A New World of Educational Requirements

A long time ago, when you and I were in school, our educational pursuits were primarily comprised of two-dimensional activities. We listened to the teacher, took notes, read books, wrote our classroom assignments on sheets of nicely lined paper, and took tests. Our homework, if any, consisted of more of the same: take your books home, read an assignment, write the answers on paper. If we were lucky, our classroom lives were enriched once or twice weekly by art instruction. Then we could pick up and draw on our pieces of paper, cut them, fold them, and paste them into new and different shapes. For some of us, that was the best part of school, perhaps the only time we felt creative, competent, and in control. Unfortunately, art class was all-too-brief, then it was back to the grind of read, write, and memorize.

INTRODUCTION

When I became a parent, I looked forward to the day when my children would start school. I used to love picking them up and always eagerly inquired about what they learned each day. Having never had any substantial homework until I was in the eighth or ninth grade, I was completely unprepared for the deluge of assignments that they received. My daughter attended a Montessori kindergarten and her first-grade teacher didn't give homework, so it wasn't until she was in second grade and my son was in kindergarten that I realized that the school experience as I had known it was history.

During the past nine years, I have retraced my education as I follow my children's progress through elementary and middle school. I have been an involved parent, at times much more involved than I wanted to be. I remember one day when I was standing with a group of mothers in the schoolyard just after the bell had rung and the children had filed into class. One of the moms turned to me and said, "So, how is your project going for Mrs. Brown?"

Without missing a beat, I responded, "Pretty good, but we still have to paint the mission walls and find some way to make the floor look like sand on the outside. I think we'll definitely get an A."

"Yeah," she responded. "We got a B last year because we forgot to label the architectural features of the buildings."

Simultaneously, we realized what we were saying. It was as if WE were in fourth grade again, trying to please the teacher.

Another mother piped up, "Well, I don't know about you, but I'm sick of Mrs. Brown giving ME homework!"

I think that was the moment that it first dawned on me. No longer are children in school on their own. These days, the parent and student are in it together. In fact, as succeeding years' projects have grown more complex and demanding, I have often wondered how any child can make it through elementary and middle school without the assistance of a tireless, well-educated, committed parent to help keep track of the various educational requirements.

INTRODUCTION

More Projects for Parents, Both Inside and Outside of School

As if your child's education weren't enough to worry about, schools now need and request assistance in many other areas that were traditionally not part of the classroom. In addition to the anticipated educational projects, which may be assigned as either in-school or at-home projects, your student will be expected to be involved in a variety of other types of projects which are intended to enhance the individual, groups within the class, the class as a whole, the school, and the community. Parents are expected to help with school activities in various ways, from volunteering your time as a helper in the classroom to offering your skills in a pseudo-teaching capacity to organizing and managing fundraisers to chaperoning field trips.

Early on in my children's education, I became one of those parents who is always at school, lingering for a few minutes or an hour at the gates, talking to other parents. I was fortunate to be self-employed for all those years, so my time was somewhat flexible. I formed friendships and soon was being asked by other parents to volunteer for this or that activity, either in the classroom or on campus. It wasn't long before I began taking more responsibility for school activities, offering to go on field trips, helping out in the classroom, and serving in offices or on committees.

I never expected to become so deeply immersed in the varied aspects of my children's educational experience. One thing simply led to another. Most of the material in this book derives from my nine years of experience as an active, concerned, and involved parent.

INTRODUCTION

As my children moved on to middle and high school, I scaled back on some of my volunteering commitments in order to pursue my writing career. I began to miss being in the schools, so I sought employment as a substitute teacher. Substituting gave me yet more insight on where kids are coming from these days, the educational standards they must meet, and how necessary interested parents are to the successful operation of today's schools. I also gained a much deeper understanding of what an extreme challenge our teachers face when they walk into their classrooms each day. But that's another book. *A Parent's Guide to School Projects* is a testimony of personal experience and observations, teacher and parent surveys, and discussions with teachers, administrators, and friends.

For those parents whose children are just starting school, I offer this book as a self-help manual. You have no idea what is in store for you and your children. As teachers seek to provide a more interactive classroom, they are increasingly relying on parents to support their children's learning in a variety of non-traditional ways. A book report is no longer a few paragraphs thrown on the page. In fact, there may be only one similarity between the book reports that you and I did and the book reports our children do: the student starts by reading a book. After that, the sky is the limit. Your child may be asked to dress as a character in the book, create a diorama or model of a favorite scene, write a play based on the story, create his or her own book, or do a Power Point presentation. And guess who is expected to create the costume, purchase the craft supplies, or make sure your child has access to a computer? Bingo! It's Mom, Dad, or whoever is responsible for the student's care.

INTRODUCTION

From cardboard to Styrofoam to clay to overhead projectors and computer programs, school as we parents experienced it is no longer the status quo. As early as second or third grade, students are expected to participate in group projects, deliver individual presentations, and, in some schools, even perform peer evaluations. By fourth or fifth grade, some schools fully expect the students to write ten to twenty page Modern Language Association (MLA) style research papers. Computer skills aren't simply a plus; they are now required for Internet research, drawing and presentation programs, many of which include tables, diagrams, and statistical measurement tools. Many teachers prefer the perfectly typed (and spell-checked) reports to the familiar handwritten, error-filled composition.

Relax – School Projects Can Be FUN!

Now that you are scared silly to even enroll your child in kindergarten, I will tell you a secret: for most parents, school projects of all types can be fun. This book offers some simple guidelines for you to follow, as you teach both yourself and your child to be prepared for just about anything. I will discuss some of the more common types of projects that your child may be expected to produce during his or her journey through elementary and middle schools (formerly known as "junior high" way back when) and give you an idea of how to cope with the performance anxiety that these projects may produce in your child (okay, in you, too).

Your child looks to you as a role model of efficiency, creativity, and enthusiasm. If you groan and make faces when projects are assigned, your child will develop that same attitude. Think how much more smoothly everything will go if you can express some genuine interest in your child's tasks, no matter how busy your schedule is. "Be prepared" is the motto you must adopt. By the time you finish this book, you will have a fully stocked school crafts cupboard, a selection of sample projects, a list of "must have" and "must plan on" items, and a willingness to guide your child through the maze of teacher expectations, peer critiques, and individual insecurities.

INTRODUCTION

You will learn to take the initiative and contact other parents whose kids are involved in a group project with your kids. You will guide your child's interpretation of the tasks of a project, help in your student's efforts to budget time and materials, and act as his personal coach and cheerleading squad as he plods through the more daunting sections of it. You will do all this with a big smile on your face because you have become aware of the educational value of the various types of projects your child is being asked to produce.

Academics and Much More

Your child is expected to faithfully complete all classroom assignments and maintain a certain level of participation in his or her school activities. But did you realize that parents are also expected to be as active and involved as possible? Besides helping your kid with homework, driving them to and from school, and providing materials and supplies for school projects, most schools clamor for parent involvement in a physical way. That's right. They want you on campus as often as possible, pitching in to make life easier for both teachers and administrators. By the time your child graduates from eighth grade, you will have devoted hours and hours of volunteer time to your school community. You will use every talent you have and discover some you didn't know you had.

INTRODUCTION

Why You Need This Book

I wrote this book because, almost as soon as my children began their journey through elementary school, I felt like I had hopped onto a moving train. Though I live in Southern California, I have friends all over the country who tell me that they had the same experience. As bright and competent and educated as my friends and I like to think we are, we were all taken by surprise at the amount of time and commitment it is taking to get our kids through school. It's not just about dropping the little ones off at 8:30 in the morning and picking them up at 3:00 in the afternoon. It's about being there as a full participant in your child's education.

Any skill or talent or job experience or hobby you have may ultimately be just what is needed and wanted for some school-sponsored event, activity, or classroom procedure. You will be challenged to stretch your imagination as you endeavor to assist your child in preparing what can seem like endless school projects. You will be required to open your pocketbook over and over for all manner of fundraisers, worthy causes, and school functions. You will be called upon to serve on committees, donate items, chaperone kids, bring or send food, and run book fairs. Your child's school will become a major focus of your attention. You will expand your notion of what it means to be a part of an educational community and do everything possible to help your own and other children to get a decent education.

I divided this book into several sections that reflect the main areas where you might need some help adjusting to the demands of educating your child. From understanding how and why your child's teachers require academic projects to instructions on running a fundraiser to stocking your at-home supplies cupboard, it's all here. I described the many types of projects, presentations, and papers that your child will be expected to produce during his or her academic career. I included an appendix of actual projects that teachers assign, as well as photos of completed projects. The book also contains a glossary of terms and a section on important educational concepts, including time management, ethics, following directions, and the art of criticism.

INTRODUCTION

Sending your child to school is a lot like having a baby. We start out thinking it must be quite simple because we all know lots of people who have done it. It seems to be a logical and somewhat ordinary human endeavor. We're pretty sure that any competent, intelligent person should be able to get through it without too much fuss. Then we bring our little darling baby home and she screams for three days straight. We call everyone we know for advice, but nothing works. That's when it hits you: you have to figure out what is right for you and your child and then do it.

Every year, your child will have a new teacher, a new set of classroom rules, and a new level of educational challenges to meet. If you move around much, your child may even encounter more than one school along the way. Ultimately, you will figure out that the only constant in your child's education is you. Read this book and you will at least know in advance some of the ways in which you can help your child, your child's teachers, your school community, and, best of all, yourself. You will be prepared for most scenarios and be able to guide both your children and other parents as they seek to make the best of their kids' educational experiences.

Chapter One

Educators Need Your Help

During the past decade or two, the classroom environment has changed immensely. Educators have realized that the simple reading and writing methods of imparting information to children don't necessarily work for all students. How many times have we heard of a child who was totally incompetent in the classroom setting, no matter how hard his teachers tried, who went on to excel in a profession that no one would have ever thought him capable of, based on his school performance? Thanks to more in-depth educational research, creative educational methods, and knowledge of different learning styles, the child who constructed elaborate buildings and sand castles, but who was unable to follow the chain of events from reading a book to writing a book report, now has a more even playing field in the classroom.

CHAPTER ONE

The changes that we observe in children's performance and comprehension are partly in response to profound differences in the culture; television, computers, and the rapidly moving economy all impact our children's expectations, as well as their ability to perform. I don't know about you, but I have definitely noticed that my children's method of processing information is incredibly different from mine. From the age of about two or three (sooner for many), they were exposed to TV screens and computer monitors. Things happen more quickly on TV than in real life. Time is compressed. Kids seem able to focus on more than one thing at a time, but actually seem distracted when asked to focus on only one thing (e.g., homework *without* music, TV, or friends in the room.)

Recently, my children were reminiscing about sitting in front of the TV as toddlers, watching Sesame Street and other educational programming during the week and on Saturday mornings. (Of course, this was before we had the Cartoon Network and Nickelodeon, which gives them access to *all cartoons, all the time*.) Suddenly, they broke into a song about conjunctions, ("Conjunction Junction, What's your function?"), from the *Schoolhouse Rock* series. It was actually a very useful song with a bouncy little melody that my kids apparently had stored for future use. They explained that they had learned this and many other learning-packed little ditties by paying attention, not only to Sesame Street, but also to the numerous educational shorts that were shown between Saturday cartoons. Suddenly, I felt a lot less guilty for letting them watch TV!

When I finally summoned the courage to use a computer, it literally took me weeks to learn how to manipulate the mouse to make the cursor move in the direction I wanted it to move on the screen. It was painful, tedious, and extremely frustrating. In contrast, children today are masters of hand-eye coordination as they use the mouse and the keyboard to play educational and entertainment games, write essays, and surf the Net for research purposes. My belief is that they have learned to access and absorb information in ways that adults, even those of us who use computers, will never understand. The classroom, with its lack of immediate gratification and intense stimulation, must be quite a shock to the nervous systems of kids who are accustomed to non-stop noise, movement, lights, and voices. It is nearly impossible for teachers to compete with the many types of

EDUCATORS NEED YOUR HELP

stimulation that the kids are subject to in every other aspect of their lives. Teachers also must regularly confront and handle sociological and psychological issues involving classroom management. Seasoned teachers will refer to a "really great class," where the kids seemed to bond and work together. I have also seen very experienced teachers roll their eyes, saying, "Oh, *that class*," and shudder when I explain which room I am teaching in that day. Within a school, teachers know which children or groupings of children are unmanageable. They sometimes mention the difficult students by name and say, "Oh, I had those two in a class last year. Good luck."

In my kids' school, there was one experienced male 5th grade teacher who had a reputation for being able to handle "difficult boys." And believe me, 5th grade boys can be a handful. Troublesome ten- and eleven-year-olds were routinely routed into his class because the administration knew he would be able to extract their cooperation with his no-nonsense, strict guidelines approach. Plus, bottom line, he was a man and boys often have more respect and/or fear for the male teachers. This is not politically correct, but it is true.

This book is not meant to review the many problems that today's teachers must work around. Suffice it to say that it is difficult for the classroom teacher to hold the children's interest by simply imparting the information to them in the traditional classroom manner. And it is difficult for them to manage children who aren't interested or can't pay attention, for whatever reason. Based on what many teachers have indicated in discussions and surveys, projects are a way of pulling the child into a three-dimensional relationship with the material. Children are accustomed to watching screens and manipulating figures on screens. They have a tendency to react to the teacher as if she were behind a screen, i.e., ignoring her or talking when she is talking, almost as if they don't realize that she can actually see them. In order to engage students in a more focused and hands-on experience, teachers have learned to be extremely creative. Parents must also be willing to stretch their creativity and expectations in order to help their children meet the teachers' criteria.

CHAPTER ONE

Teachers' Views

Most teachers whom I have met and talked to are dedicated and eager to bring out the best in all students. Considering the amount of work they are expected to do and the meager pay scale, they certainly aren't teaching for the money! Many teachers feel hampered by the school administrations' emphasis on test scores and performance assessments. They often complain that it seems like they are continually preparing children for one or another test, with little time left over to give the children latitude to learn in different ways. A fair percentage of the teachers I have interviewed admit that, though they would love to do projects, they simply do not have the time to do them. Other teachers say that they assign their students as many as five large projects and 15 smaller projects in a school year.

It is fair to say that some subjects lend themselves to projects more easily than others. For example, Social Studies, History, English, and Science are subjects that provide a wealth of information on which to base projects. Surprisingly, some math teachers manage to come up with interesting project ideas, including enlarging objects and forming classroom banks.

My children have been assigned projects (both group and individual) from teachers of language, computers, health, life skills, and even ceramics. Everything depends on the teacher's ability to extend the learning environment to encompass and inspire the students' creativity.

Most Effective Projects

Most teachers have a pet project that they assign year after year, one that they feel meets the curriculum while allowing the students some leeway to express their learning and to use abilities not limited to reading and writing. In many schools, these projects become legendary. Children in lower grades look forward

Some of the projects that teachers refer to time and again in my local district (Southern California) include:
- 4th grade: Social studies reports dealing with local or state history. (In California, the Mission and/or Native American projects).
- 5th grade: The U.S. state report.
- 6th Grade: Reports on Greek and Roman culture.
- 7th Grade: The Middle Ages project.
- 8th Grade: The Civil War project.
- K-8: Various science projects.
- All grades: The book report (the universal standby, many variations).

EDUCATORS NEED YOUR HELP

to the day when they will reach the fourth or fifth grade and be able to do the big project that they watched their older siblings complete. Students love such projects because they are seen as a milestone in the child's education. Teachers love them because they are effective in accomplishing the teacher's overall educational goals.

Primary teachers tend to love projects that open the child's world to nature and promote that inherent sense of wonder commonly seen among the five-to-eight crowd. They are also masters of turning anything from toilet paper rolls to oatmeal boxes and egg crates to some marvelous secondary use. (Be prepared to recycle!)

What the Teacher Wants

Photo by Sierra Weir

Humanity, **Lord of the Flies** Theme collage by Brett Weir, Grade 6

When teachers assign academic projects, they are looking for the same general results. Some teachers are mostly interested in teaching the child to follow directions. Other projects are designed to teach the child to generate an original idea within broader guidelines. I have seen situations where the teacher asked for a 3-5 page paper with a project and actually took points away from a student whose paper was 6 pages long. Since the teacher decides the emphasis of the project and also delivers the grade, it is always wise to have your student clarify any points of confusion with the teacher *before* starting the project.

For the most part, the teacher wants to see genuine effort on the part of his or her students in both understanding and executing the project. They also want to see evidence of a methodical and systematic approach to producing an excellent product (see Chapter Eight for more details regarding project management). In a language class, the underlying purpose of the project might be the development of speaking skills when the child demonstrates or describes the project or delivers the report to her classmates. Other objectives could involve helping the child to broaden his or her knowledge of cultures in which the language is spoken or to gain a sense of where the country is located geographically or what natural resources are available.

CHAPTER ONE

In a science class, the teacher is usually interested in ascertaining that the child understands the scientific method that rules all scientific experimentation. For the English teacher, the most important part of the project might be the way in which the student demonstrates how he or she processed the words of the author. For example, a teacher will sometimes ask a student to create a collage or model of the theme of a book he read. She is interested in seeing whether the child interpreted the language and context of the book into a mental picture that was then translated back into the physical model. Until you have seen the range of interpretations that arise from a single story or novel, you may not understand how rewarding such a project can be to a teacher.

In group projects, the teachers hope for cooperation and mutual encouragement. More often, teachers find themselves refereeing amongst egos the size of Ohio, with tears flowing and tempers flaring. In the end, if the project survives the many disputes, the children will have learned something about how to control themselves long enough to contribute to the group and produce a shared project. Mind you, even the best of friends can end up not talking when a bad grade results. Many teachers actually assign different parts of a project to different group members, then grade each student according to his or her assigned section. They use the group model as a learning tool for the students' sake, but don't actually give a group grade. Students are usually not given this information up front.

Methods of Learning

In the past few years, much has been written about the different types of intelligences that are operant in the range of human abilities; from spatial abilities to analytical and reasoning skills to emotional IQ, we each have our strengths and weaknesses. We are not all brilliant writers or math whizzes, and we don't all absorb information in the same way.

I remember walking into my son's kindergarten class one day to find his teacher reading *Seven Pathways of Learning: Teaching Students and Parents about Multiple Intelligences,* by David Lazear. She smiled and said, "I'm learning about your son's mind." She'd had some problems convincing him to do two-dimensional work. He only wanted to build elaborate structures out of Legos or play with the Math Game (where the numbers were weighted so that if you put two numbers on one side, their sum would balance it on the other). Though he was clearly perform-

EDUCATORS NEED YOUR HELP

ing at grade level and showed an eagerness to learn, he was fairly resistant to doing it "her way." Like many other teachers, she had figured out that students who seem disinterested or uncooperative in the classroom may actually simply be unsuited to learning via the traditional classroom methods. She ultimately learned that if she rewarded him often by allowing him to go to the "Lego Center" or "Math Center" as soon as he completed his written work, he was more than willing to go with the flow. Bless teachers like her for finding ways to let our children shine.

A student who is terrified to raise his hand in class may possess a gift for painting or drawing. When he is given the opportunity to do a project that involves more artistic skills, his self-esteem will soar. Perhaps you have a more mechanically-minded student who has trouble with grammar, but can design a scientific model of the solar system complete with moving parts that emulate the actual journeys of planets around the sun. Imagine her excitement when she wins the award for best science project.

Most of the teachers I talked to or who filled out surveys for me shared one common goal: they want *all* of their students to have the opportunity to explore all aspects of their creativity, intelligence, and capabilities. To encourage and sponsor this excellence, teachers go out of their way to design new and different school projects that allow each child to be an individual and learn in whatever way is comfortable and most productive. For most teachers, stepping out of the traditional mode of teaching means putting in more effort themselves, usually on their own time and often at their own expense.

Science teachers in particular are known for dedicating hours and hours of extra effort to tutoring children in their yearly science projects. Organizing science fairs and recruiting judges to evaluate the students' projects all take time and planning. Particularly in middle school, where the winning projects are sent on to the county and possibly the state level, science teachers must coordinate additional paperwork and schedule time away from the classroom to assist their protégés as they venture into the more competitive world of science projects. Each year at the State Science Fair in L.A. County, several teachers are given awards for their excellence in mentoring students' science projects over a period of time. Nominations are made by the students themselves.

CHAPTER ONE

How Parents Can Help

Like teachers, most parents want their children to do well. The problem is, they don't always know how to help or even if they should help. During my entire career as a student from kindergarten through high school, I don't ever recall asking either of my parents for help with my homework. That is not to say I didn't need it sometimes. It just never occurred to me to ask. I fully expected that my children would go to school, do their homework, and never need and/or want to ask for my help. *Was I wrong!* These days, it is not only common for children to ask for help, teachers and school administrators expect parents to help.

Starting from kindergarten, your child will be bringing home interactive assignments and projects which, at the very least, require your signature. Some mini-projects require the child to interview you or have you fill out a survey at the end with questions such as "What did you think of this assignment?" or "How did your child react to doing it?" and "Do you have suggestions regarding how this assignment could be improved." There is a definite implication in such documents that the parent is expected to be involved in what the child is doing.

It is natural to want to help your child do his best, but too often parents get caught up in attempts to cajole, manipulate, or threaten the student into getting things done at home. In the long run, the parent is actually conditioning the child to need that type of input to accomplish anything. In other words, the more you push, the less the student will accomplish. Believe me, I've been there.

Since projects require much more attention and planning than the normal homework duties, it is probably best if you begin to help your child pace himself as soon as he begins getting homework assignments (i.e., kindergarten or first grade). This involves having a quiet, well-lit, non-distracting work space in your home, with a set time period during which the child is expected to complete his assignments each night. During the early years, it is fairly easy to assist your child by picking up where the teacher left off in teaching. Small rewards may be helpful, but beware of letting your child think that he or she is *owed* something for every little successful completion.

Despite my college degrees, I have found that helping with homework is not as easy as it sounds. For example, children are advancing through math at a faster rate than we did. They are now tackling pre-Algebra and Algebra in sixth and

EDUCATORS NEED YOUR HELP

seventh grades. In order to be competent to help them, I found I had to relearn the concepts; I then realized I was way too disinterested to do that, so I got them a tutor. If you find that your help is actually more of a hindrance to your child, I suggest you back off. Find a friend or family member to pick up the slack, or sign junior up for after-school tutoring. Stick with helping in the areas where you can actually contribute to the child's store of knowledge.

This book isn't really about helping with homework per se. I mention it only because the habits and attitudes your child develops about homework in general will extend to his or her ability to tackle school projects. If you start early to teach your child the basics of doing good, timely, complete, and competent work, the leap to projects will be smoothly accomplished. You will already have developed a good working relationship with your child and your help will be welcome, not burdensome. Most important, you will already know your child's strengths and weaknesses and will be able to successfully guide him or her to select a project that builds on those qualities, allowing your child to achieve maximum success in each project.

Reaching Every Child

Children learn at different rates and in different ways. For example, some students can recall what they read almost verbatim. Others recall nothing of what they read without taking copious notes. As a student, if I didn't take notes during a lecture, I came away with very little information. But if I not only took notes in class, but typed them as soon as I got home, the material was as much a part of my own knowledge as if I had originated it. In contrast, my daughter actually seems to lose information if she takes notes. She recalls things better simply from listening to what was said, rather than from writing it down.

If your child hates to hand write essays, the problem may be one of fine motor control. Ask the teacher if she could be allowed to type it instead. If the problem goes deeper, i.e., your child "just can't think of anything to say," you will have to determine whether that is simply an excuse not to do the work or she actually doesn't get the material. Talk to the teacher about how you can assist in improving her reading comprehension or motivate her to complete the assignments.

CHAPTER ONE

Photo by Sierra Weir

Drawing stimulates learning – Calendar Project by Brett Weir

What about the child who wants to sit and doodle all day, but can't seem to formulate an idea in writing? One partial answer to that dilemma is the storyboard. Students can now draw something that resembles a cartoon to explain what they learned in the story they are reading. They still have to fill little bubbles with character dialogue. The main idea is to demonstrate an understanding of the material. While this method can't replace the traditional essay or book report, it can at least give the teacher an idea of whether the student absorbed any information from the book. It also gives the student whose drawing skills are superior to his writing skills a better chance at expressing his understanding of the text.

A child may not even know why or how he is unable to express certain concepts in the traditional manner. Computers have proven to be very valuable learning tools because they can give the child immediate feedback on right or wrong answers, along with visual and sound cues that tend to trigger memory using different parts of the brain. Schools are now using computers to assist in teaching, starting in kindergarten and progressing all the way through high school.

Ask your child's teacher where you can buy educational games that are identical or similar to the ones used in the classroom. Stock up on that software and let your child practice learning concepts and skills on your home computer. Take the time to learn how your child learns. Talk to the teacher about options for enhancing his learning style. Read everything you can that helps you understand both your child's needs and his teachers' educational goals.

How to Support Teachers and Administrators

Without the ongoing assistance of parents, teachers and administrators would have a much more difficult time educating our children. Beyond the direct academic help that your child needs and deserves, you can lend support to your child's teachers and school administration by actively participating in all school activities, including volunteering as a classroom helper, chaperoning off-campus trips and events, organizing and running fund raisers, serving on the school committees and on parent-teacher organization boards, and offering to help out with any other school-sponsored projects and activities. These opportunities are more fully discussed in Chapters Six and Seven.

Chapter Two

Individual Academic Projects

Purpose

Teachers assign academic projects for various reasons. For one thing, it creates a "workshop" environment within the classroom, which changes the way students approach the subject. Individual students are given an opportunity to demonstrate and apply their knowledge three-dimensionally, using different mediums and methods of creative expression. Some projects that your child will be required to complete will come with a specific set of instructions requiring nearly absolute compliance. Such projects may include the annual science project, which must follow the standard scientific method; certain math projects, such as enlarging an object; and the rocket building (and firing) project.

CHAPTER TWO

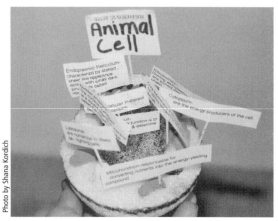

Photo by Shana Kordich

An Animal Cell in Three Dimensions, Science project by Ian Kordich, 7th Grade Dodson Middle School, RPV, CA

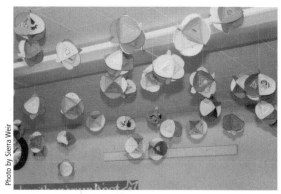

Photo by Sierra Weir

Constructing Octahedrons, a project that requires students to follow strict directions. By Joyce Kimura, 7th Grade Math teacher, Dodson Gifted & High Ability Magnet Middle School, RPV, CA

Directions that students bring home for other projects may be so vague as to seem incomprehensible at first glance. These are more likely to be humanities projects (art, social studies, English), where the directions are considered to be guidelines or taking-off points. In the latter type of projects, students are expected to interpret, extrapolate, and expand the directions to express their individual creativity and ingenuity, while still staying within the basic context of what the teacher wanted. Regardless of the type of project assigned, teachers are generally going to evaluate them based on similar guidelines, i.e., Did the student follow directions? Are all aspects of the project complete? And was the project handed in on time?

Of course, your child will also be graded on the project's content, presentation, and level of sophistication. But no matter how complicated or well-executed a project may be, if it is off-topic, incomplete in any way, or late, the grade will be significantly lower than what the student had hoped for. Help your child keep those three criteria in mind when he is working on any project for any teacher, and you will keep him on the path to pleasing the teacher and earning the grade he strives for.

INDIVIDUAL ACADEMIC PROJECTS

Learning Through Doing

If you've ever taught school or been a room mother or classroom assistant, you probably have seen the amazing metamorphosis that occurs when children switch from regular classroom work to some activity that involves cutting, pasting, folding, or otherwise manipulating paper or other materials with their hands. Children can be staring off into space, half awake, clearly not paying attention, but when they hear the magic words, "Now put your books away. We're going to work on our Valentine's Day cards for mom and dad," you can feel the surge of energy in the room.

Children who a few minutes before looked positively catatonic are now busily handing out papers and crayons, listening eagerly for directions, measuring paper, and planning a beautiful and creative work of art. And although some of their projects might not always show it, as they measure and cut and paste, they are absorbing the concepts of color combination, design, formatting, and layout.

I was recently substituting in a second grade classroom where the teacher had left 5x8-inch squares of about 25 different colors of paper. Each student was given a cutout black mask and was only allowed to choose four other colors with which to decorate it. I don't think any two students chose the same set of colors. And the masks, though each started on the same black paper cut into the same size and shape, were startlingly original in form, concept, and design. Each child had expressed him or herself non-verbally, with exquisite originality. The best part was they were all having fun, they helped each other make choices and decisions, and they were all happy with their results.

Projects pull the children closer to what they are doing through the senses of touch and smell. If they cut out something and it isn't quite right, they can look at the problem and make a new plan. For some reason, anything that they identify with "playing" or "having fun," i.e., anything that they

CHAPTER TWO

used to do at home or in preschool before they got stuck sitting at desks and writing or reading all day, suddenly frees them to make mistakes. A child who will go rigid in fear at the thought of writing a sentence will happily cut out nose after nose to put on his mask until he "gets it right." Projects, the merging of the abstract intention with the actual manipulation of objects and materials, somehow bridges the academic abyss that some children seem to fall into in elementary school.

Photo by Sierra Weir

The Best Little Girl in the World, Book Report Display Board by Danica Nizich, Linda Velasco's 8th Grade English class, Dodson Gifted and High Ability Magnet Middle School, RPV, CA

Just the other day, a teacher who had assigned a book report/visual display project was pointing out some of the incredible details that the students had incorporated into their posters. Some had added three-dimensional characters that were fastened to the board, yet weren't exactly part of it. One child had added net curtains to the board as a background for a ballet dancer. Another student had made a house-shaped book – each successive page added a new aspect of analysis to the report. The teacher said she hadn't asked them for that much detail, but she was always amazed at the amount of work some students would put into their projects. I asked her if she learned a lot about some of them from the way they implemented her directions. She said yes. Then she added that many students who excelled on the usual classroom work in "black and white" didn't always produce the most visually interesting projects, while others, whose classroom work was less stellar, absolutely stunned her with their creative efforts on projects.

INDIVIDUAL ACADEMIC PROJECTS

Learning Through Teaching Peers

Photo by Sierra Weir

The Diary of Anne Frank, Character Wheel Book Report Display, by Garrett Brill, Linda Velasco's 8th Grade English class, Dodson Gifted and High Ability Magnet Middle School, RPV, CA

When a child is called upon to present or explain his or her project to the class, something magical happens. The child becomes a junior teacher. Other children ask questions and learn from the presenting child. Each child in turn has a chance to share his or her knowledge about a particular subject. Children learn about and from one another. This builds confidence in the individual child, as well as in the group.

I have taught in classes where the children have clearly become a group who are learning together and who are committed to helping one another learn. As each child takes his or her turn reciting a poem or explaining how he or she assembled the social studies model, the others learn to be polite and receptive. They know that each one of them will have to walk up front and deliver a similar talk, so they learn the value of being an audience. The children also begin to understand what the teacher is experiencing as she tries to keep everyone focused on what she is saying. If one or two of the children who are supposed to be listening begin to chat, the other students shush them and demand that they be polite.

Another outcome of allowing the child to teach is that the child relearns the subject. I think we've all had the experience of gaining a better understanding of an idea or subject when we have to explain it to someone else. This is one of the foundations of learning. In effect, the child is reteaching himself as he informs the other students.

CHAPTER TWO

Learning Through Evaluating Peers' Work

In some schools, children are assigned individual projects, which are in turn evaluated by the rest of the students in the class. This can be nerve-wracking to the sensitive or less popular child. In an ideal setting, i.e., one in which the students are committed to every other student's success and where they have learned to give positive criticism, the peer evaluation can add to the child's understanding of the impact of her project among her peers. A teacher who can achieve this level of group support and encouragement is definitely correct in promoting such interactive evaluations.

Unfortunately, I have seen this aspect of project evaluation go terribly wrong. In all cases, I believe the teachers had the best of intentions, seeking to expand the children's horizons and prepare them for the inevitable college and workplace experiences. However, in fourth and fifth grade, many children are simply not ready to be judged by a group, particularly if the guiding principles seem to be popularity and conformity instead of excellence and educational performance. My personal belief is that most children under fourteen are not emotionally equipped to contend with the experience of presenting one's project to the class, only to have other children either vote or otherwise comment on the success of one's efforts.

In fairness to teachers, they are mostly aware of the bias of students' reactions, and they have the final say on the actual grade. Teachers have told me that the standard reaction of poking fun and trying to trip up the less popular students by asking far-fetched questions are exactly the types of behaviors that they are trying to discourage by conducting peer evaluations. I believe that teachers intend to achieve a long-term goal of acceptance that fosters constructive criticism and improves goals. For that reason, I have tried to be supportive, even as I am dragging my child into the classroom when it is her day to be evaluated, even when she comes home crying because so-and-so made fun of her costume or said her model looked crooked. Even then.

INDIVIDUAL ACADEMIC PROJECTS

The good side of peer evaluations is that your child can learn a lot about how *not* to do it. You can teach the Golden Rule simply by saying, "When you comment on Johnny's project, make sure to say what you really like first, and then talk about what you might change." Or not. I'm writing this as a heads-up for parents. You will have to find a way to help your child accept and deliver peer evaluations because they have become an accepted practice in many schools. Short of homeschooling or making your child into a complete outsider by not allowing her to participate in certain activities, you'll just have to find a "glass-half-filled" approach to helping your kids get through them.

Mom and Me

Let's face it, until you have helped your child unpack in his college dormitory room, you will be involved in school projects. In the primary grades, you will be actively supporting, coaching, and guiding the project, helping your little one to learn the necessary steps to a successfully executed stuffed bumble bee or a cardboard fire-engine with movable parts. As your child proceeds through the last two years of elementary school (currently fourth and fifth grades), you should see an increased awareness and ability in planning and following through on the projects, but your student will still need your help in keeping the project within time and budget constraints.

By the time the middle school years roll around, provided you have taken an active role in the preceding years, your child should be ready to plan fully and execute a project with minimal parental involvement. Well, they should at least be able to do all the research, writing, and organizing. You will probably still be called upon to go to the store, help find pictures in magazines, search the house for materials and artifacts, surf the Internet for facts and figures, and troubleshoot the computer program when the A-drive won't open the disk that your student brought home from school (this usually happens around 10 p.m. the night before the project is due). In fact, this A-drive nightmare scenario happened to me just last year, when my daughter was in eighth grade. Her little disk refused to open no matter what we did.

CHAPTER TWO

Lucky for us, bits and pieces of her paper were still extant on the hard drive and she had gotten her illustrations off the Internet. So there we were, at 2:00 a.m., bleary-eyed and snapping at each other, trying to recreate her six-page paper. We managed to finish it, threats and dire warnings notwithstanding.

What I'm trying to say is that no matter how independent, brilliant, and energetic your student is, he or she will rely on you to inspire those great project ideas. By making yourself available to your child, you will expand your own knowledge and forge an unbreakable bond with your child. Don't be surprised at how much you enjoy the experience of helping your child with projects.

You need HOW MUCH?
Choosing a project that fits your resources and your child's interests

Many times, our children's creative and inventive ideas do not match our pocketbooks. When little Mario comes home with an idea for a science project that involves ordering a hundred dollars' worth of gizmos from a science fair catalogue, it's time for a talk. Sometimes, the student has a great idea that can be scaled down. For example, instead of building a full-size vehicle that runs on water instead of gasoline, let's just build a scale prototype of the engine. Or how about a *replica* of a Native American teepee instead of one that Johnny and three friends can sleep in after he gets his grade? Convincing your student to scale down the project doesn't necessarily mean that you are shutting down his creativity. It can actually be an exercise in common sense, whereby the child learns about the need to inject a little practicality into his creative vision.

INDIVIDUAL ACADEMIC PROJECTS

It is also important to keep your child grounded in terms of who exactly is going to help her accomplish her grandiose plan. You may be lucky and have a huge extended family that includes carpenters, engineers, scientists, gardening experts, graphic artists, and computer geniuses. Or you may be a single parent, struggling to keep up with your many responsibilities and limited time. Item number one on the student's "to-do" list might be finding the right person to help manage the project. If neither parent nor child can think of a helpful resource person, then that would be a good time to refocus the project. The more thinking that is done up front, the less crying will be endured later on.

On the other hand, never be afraid to ask for help. I have enlisted support from friends, neighbors, grandparents, and co-workers. If someone in your circle of friends and relatives is an expert on World War II, then get on the phone and have him or her take little Abbey on a tour of museums and libraries to gather that important background data for her project. People love to be needed, especially if it gives them a chance to share their knowledge with a thirsty little mind. My children's grandparents are always a great source for project ideas and materials. They have provided Native American artifacts, including baskets, grinding stones (matate), and arrowheads; various types of rocks and gem stones; photos and paintings of ancestors; ancient coins; antique quilts, books on many subjects; and animal skulls.

Photos by Sierra Weir

Found at Grandma and Grandpa's house: Navajo wedding basket, Two Grey Wolves Zuni Rug (above). Native American artifacts: grinding stone (matate)

CHAPTER TWO

Helping Your Student Understand Project Parameters

Nothing is more stressful to a parent than a child who is agonizing over a pending project. While a certain amount of anxiety over a looming deadline is normal, there is a point at which the anxiety will overshadow the possible benefits of the learning experience and put the child in a no-win situation. This may lead to procrastination and/or an overall feeling of hopelessness on your child's part. You need to be able to identify the signs that your child is getting overwrought and successfully defuse your child's anxiety. A few simple precautions on your part will do wonders to minimize your child's trepidations while maximizing productivity.

If your child comes home, throws his backpack on the floor, and collapses in tears on the couch, and the only words you can make out are "project due" and "don't understand what the teacher wants," it's time for you to put on your mentor hat and carefully get at the truth. Remember, your child may be focused only on the due date, the number of possible points to be earned, or the rumors from last year's students about how hard that teacher grades *that* project. So, the most important first act: ask to see the assignment. This may involve the dreaded backpack search, which could yield anything from last week's yogurt container to the $5 bill he supposedly lost, not to mention several mangled documents that you were supposed to sign and return two months ago. Okay, so your kid's backpack is immaculate and everything is in order (lucky you), whatever.

If your child says he lost or can't find or never saw the project outline, it's time to call a friend, a friend's mother, and/or the teacher. Do anything you have to, but find the paper. Trust me, I've been through this scenario several times. You will generally find that your child has built up an anxiety that is all out of proportion to what is written on the page. A note of hope here: we live in an age of fax machines, e-mails, and homework hotlines. It's entirely possible to retrieve lost assignments without ever calling the teacher or visiting the school.

INDIVIDUAL ACADEMIC PROJECTS

Finally, you've excavated Tommy's room and located the project assignment. Sit down with your child when he's not tired and carefully review what it says. Usually, the teacher will have broken down the tasks into bite-sized portions, precisely because he or she *does* understand how children's minds work. If the total project is worth 200 points, the teacher may assign 10 points for neatness, 50 for content, 40 for getting the first draft in on time, 5 for the introduction, 5 for each illustration, etc.

Probably the most important thing for your student to grasp is that he or she has *plenty* of time to complete all aspects of the project, provided that he or she plans carefully and doesn't procrastinate. Grab a calendar and mark off today's date and the date the project is due. In my experience, students may have as much as four to six weeks advance notice on humanities projects (e.g., English, social studies, history, Spanish, etc.) and up to 3-4 months for science projects in middle school.

We've all struggled through those last-minute papers and projects. If you're wise, you will not allow your child to delay starting his project with the familiar excuses: "It's all done except for the little paragraphs I have to write," or "I'm pretty sure she didn't want us to color it in," or "I can't start cutting the cardboard until I decide what color to make the inside of the castle," etc. Buy a whiteboard or simply hang a poster in your child's room. Then make a prioritized list of what needs to be done, so that both of you have a visual concept of how far along the project really is.

One of my daughter's teachers included a "Project Planning Sheet" with every project. You can copy it from the Appendix (pg. 201). If you *really* want to score some points with your child's teachers, make about 100 copies and distribute them to the teachers at the beginning of the year. They will love you. However you decide to do it, it is extremely important to keep your child on track with projects. Trust me, if you wait until the night before, you will be the one putting the final touches on the project while your child sleeps peacefully in the next room.

CHAPTER TWO

Budgeting Time

Help your child decide how much time he or she feels is necessary to complete each smaller part of the project. For example, drawing a map or illustrating an invertebrate will take less time than doing the primary research for the written report. Grab a calendar and write in the days and times when the student will have to visit the library or reserve time on the family computer to do research. Make a list of all the necessary supplies: poster board, colored pencils, construction paper, three-dimensional display materials. If you don't already have most of them in your home (see Chapter Eight), then you will be shopping for them.

If you live close enough to a museum or other facility that will add to your child's knowledge of the subject he or she is reporting on, schedule a visit. Take a disposable camera and let him snap as many photos as possible. Encourage him to ask the docents questions and take notes on what he learns.

The last time we were in Bozeman, Montana, we toured the Gibson Guitar Factory. Now we have plenty of information on hand in case anyone in the family ever needs to write a report on how guitars are manufactured. When we visited Europe, we collected postcards and brochures and historical tracts at every museum and castle and church we visited, just in case. We also took two or three rolls of film of the last solar eclipse of the century (August, 1999) in Austria. Lo and behold, when my son's science project rolled around in May 2000 and he just *couldn't think* of an idea, he suddenly recalled that experience. (Okay, I *reminded* him of it – he'll never admit to that). We bought a few different-sized Styrofoam balls. He rigged some wire and a block of wood, researched Encarta and a few Internet sites, whipped up a paper, stapled the photos to the board, and *Voila!* he had a science project "What Happens During a Solar Eclipse?"

Photo by Sierra Weir

Display board for Solar Eclipse Science Project

INDIVIDUAL ACADEMIC PROJECTS

What if your child has to choose a state for a state project (generally done in fourth or fifth grade)? Usually, the teacher requests that you don't do a project on the state you live in, but otherwise, the choice is open. Make things a bit easier. Suggest that little Elliott do a report on the state you grew up in or choose one where your relatives still reside. My son chose to do his report on Montana, because by the time he was in 5th grade, we had visited Montana every summer since he was two. He thought of it as a familiar place. Maybe you live close enough to the border between your state and the next to actually take a little family outing to that state. If all else fails, help your child write a letter to his chosen state's information and tourist bureau to obtain brochures, travel guides, and economic information. These days, I suspect such requests can also be sent via e-mail.

Believe it or not, once your child relaxes into a self-generated schedule to support the project, he or she will begin to show enthusiasm for completing it. One of the key items teachers mentioned regarding why they assign projects was time management. No matter how bright or capable a student is, if he or she doesn't learn to budget time, the outcome is not promising. No doubt you have already learned to juggle schedules, assign priorities, and manage not only your own, but your children's time. When you teach your child to manage his or her time around the demands of an important school project, you are bestowing upon that child the key to future control of his or her career and life. Remember that the next time you are passing the Elmer's glue to your 10-year-old at 9 p.m. on Sunday night.

CHAPTER TWO

Transporting Displays and Paraphernalia

Speaking of the night before the project is due: be sure to figure out ahead of time who is going to help little Ricky get his project to school in the morning. Although many of us who live in Southern California are accustomed to driving our kids to school, there are still a lot of kids out there either taking buses or walking. If the display board is as tall as your child is, or if he already has a load of books in his backpack, plus his lunch to carry, how is he going to manage the board and the six potted plants? Sometimes, schools allow students to set up their projects at school, with their parents' help, on the night *before* the science fair begins. Make sure you read the science fair report guidelines before the day the project is due (see sample guidelines in the Appendix) or call the school. There's nothing sadder than a smashed science project abandoned a couple of blocks from school because your kid dropped it. Science projects should never be so complex or fragile that the student can't set it unassisted or fix any little problems *by himself*. Remember, Mom, you won't always be there to help. He has to do it himself sometime.

Kindergarten through Third Grade Projects

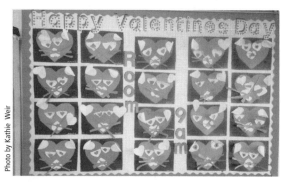

Photo by Kathie Weir

Valentine's Day Bulletin Board, Charlotte Murai's Kindergarten Class, White Point School, San Pedro, CA

Your student's very first project will probably be assigned in kindergarten and may be completed in school. It could take the form of a simple cut-and-paste art project or an elementary play performed at a school assembly. You may be asked to volunteer to cut out 20 sets of construction paper pieces to be used in making the students' first calendar or timeline.

INDIVIDUAL ACADEMIC PROJECTS

Or your child may come home with a couple of lines that he or she needs to recite in the performance. If you have any special talents, I am sure you have duly revealed them at the kindergarten orientation. You will answer the phone one day and agree to sew a few pieces of felt and cotton into a semblance of costumes or paint the backdrop for "Jack & The Beanstalk." Such activities may seem simple at first. But remember, the parent who helps once is automatically moved to the top of that teacher's "helper list." Opportunities to "help" grow exponentially as the year progresses. Before you know it, you are room mom or room dad and you are the one doing the calling. But relax, that's a bit down the road.

Back to kindergarten: a favorite primary activity involves growing beans or alfalfa sprouts in a little plastic cup of soil. If your child is lucky enough to attend a school where the kindergarteners have some space outside (in the form of a patio or separate enclosed area), their projects may extend to the outdoors. A couple of the dads in my son's kindergarten built an elaborate pyramid style wooden planter that consisted of graduated wooden boxes. The children were able to partake in a long-term garden-growing experience, where they actually were able to harvest vegetables.

Of course, the teacher was able to execute that project with the help of dad volunteers who supplied the wood, the soil, and the expertise, as well as a couple of moms who were willing to volunteer seeds, little garden tools, and lots of time. And don't forget, the mild climate helps. In colder climates, such projects might be carried out on a smaller scale inside, with growing lights, or in the spring only. Either way, you can see how valuable parents would be in this endeavor. And what a learning opportunity is thus provided to your little group of inquiring minds.

Other early childhood projects help cement basic concepts in the students' learning process. For weeks, my kindergartner brought home a brown lunch bag with a different number on the outside of it each night. His assignment involved putting the designated number of items into the bag, counting as he went. Another variation of this learning project is to put a letter on the outside of the bag, or a letter and number. For example, little Joshua might

CHAPTER TWO

be asked to find four items that begin with "L." Parents will naturally have to guide this process because, while most children will select toys and other items from their rooms, there may be the occasional little whiz who decides to search your jewelry box for diamonds to satisfy his "D" letter.

And don't forget the dreaded science project, which now begins in kindergarten. (I swear I went all the way through high school and never had to even think about a science project). With the help of a list distributed by the teacher, children come up with intriguing scientific questions such as "How much salt do you have to add to water to make an egg float?" or "Does a plant grow faster with or without light?" or "What types of objects can a magnet pick up?" Now begins the training in scientific methodology: question; hypothesis; materials; procedure; results; and, most important, "who helped me and what they did."

In kindergarten and first grade, we see an emphasis on helping the child conceptualize him- or herself as an individual, a person who comes from somewhere, who is part of a family, a school, a community, and a nation. A popular program which many, many teachers employ is the "Star of the Week" or "Student of the Week" poster. Each week, a different student is granted the honor and responsibility of preparing a poster that introduces himself or herself to the class. The poster contains information about the student's family, pets, likes and dislikes, future plans, friends, and favorite activities. Photos are included and, sometimes, the student may bring a toy, trophy, or other possession that helps define who he or she is.

Photo by Sierra Weir

Star of the Week Poster

INDIVIDUAL ACADEMIC PROJECTS

Parents, be prepared! Find out the details ahead of time. Usually the teacher will send home a list giving your student the dates of his or her special week. Drop by the classroom and look at what the other students have presented. As your student's week approaches, go through family photos and pick out a few favorites. Make sure little Ashley has written her paragraph about herself and gathered her cherished objects *before* the Monday morning when her week starts. By the way, the "Star of the Week" activity may continue through the fifth grade. So don't toss the poster after first grade. If you construct it correctly, you can always reuse the board and the background construction paper; perhaps even recycle some of the photos, adding new ones, of course. And keep the "Who I Am" or "All About Me" paragraph on a disk somewhere, so your student can revise it as he or she sees fit.

Art and music lessons are always popular in the early grades. My grandmother taught kindergarten - sixth grade for fifty years. Her old contracts and evaluations reveal that elementary school teachers used to be required to demonstrate an ability in art and/or play an instrument (preferably the piano) before being granted a teaching credential. That is no longer true, and I have watched sadly as beautiful pianos sat idly in classrooms because the teacher couldn't play. On the bright side, though, we have many talented parents who are willing to pick up the slack in that area. If you are a parent with some singing or dancing experience, or if you can play an instrument or wield a paintbrush, let the teacher know. You could lead informal music or art classes.

Photo by Sierra Weir

Art to Grow On Project by Sierra Weir

There is a great program in place in California schools called "Art to Grow On," whereby a team of parents are trained as docents to lead four original and creative art lessons to all students in an elementary school each year. This is good both for parents who may not have had much art training in their lives, as well as for students, who not only learn about different artists' methods and media, but get to emulate that artist's approach.

CHAPTER TWO

Fourth and Fifth Grade Projects

As children progress through elementary school, their projects become more challenging. Fourth grade started with a bang for my daughter. The second weekend of school, she was assigned to do a one-page report about a national symbol and create a model of that symbol. She chose the bald eagle. I still have her bald eagle model, which she carefully sculpted from clay, then baked and painted. I think this was the first project she had ever had assigned over a weekend. I expected she would offer a lot of resistance, but she was so interested in doing the model that she didn't offer any complaints, just did it.

Photos by Sierra Weir

Bald Eagle Sculpture by Sierra Weir (above). Dwelling of Juanen Native Americans of San Juan Capistrano Mission, by Jay Kordich. From Eunice Morita's 4th Grade White Point School, San Pedro, CA

Fourth and fifth grade projects tend to have a lot of parts. There seems to be a great deal of emphasis on originality and creativity. While studying the Native American tribes of California, my daughter's fourth grade class was required to build models of either one of the dwellings of the native peoples or models of some of the artifacts they used in their daily lives.

My daughter became interested in assembling a stick and straw baby carrier that women either carried on their backs or propped against a tree, with baby snugly swaddled in. She also learned about twined baskets and immediately had an urge to produce a

INDIVIDUAL ACADEMIC PROJECTS

couple of those. Actually, we learned that they were much harder to make than they appeared. I think between the two of us, we ended up twining about a 4-5 inch diameter circle, which would have been the center of the bottom of a basket, had we ever finished it. The upside of that failed project was that my daughter realized how long and hard these women must have worked to make baskets wound tightly enough to carry water.

Model of woven grass and stick baby carrier used by Native Americans in California. From Eunice Morita's 4th Grade White Point School, San Pedro, CA

Photo by Sierra Weir

One of my personal favorite elementary school projects extended for six weeks in each of the fourth and fifth grades. Our school was close enough to a marine mammal care center for the children to walk over and participate in hands-on science lessons about the ocean and its creatures. Once a week, they trekked about a mile or so to the center, where experienced teachers guided them through various experiments. They ended up compiling notebooks that recorded their observations. That project involved only one requirement for the parents: chaperone the kids on their walks, then sit in on and facilitate the workshops. Oh, and make sure your own kid finished her unit report.

CHAPTER TWO

Middle School Projects

Science Projects

Science projects begin in kindergarten and become progressively more demanding through the higher elementary grades and middle school grades. The good news is that children are required to adhere to the scientific method, no matter how simple their project is. By the time they are in fourth or fifth grade, they pretty much know that their experiments will follow a certain progression of steps that must be accurately documented and clearly stated. For those like me, who never did a science project during school, here is everything you need to know.

The purpose of a science project is to help your student develop an understanding of the scientific method. All science projects start with a *question*. In the lower grades, your child will be handed a list of simple questions that form the basis of experiments which they will be able to accomplish easily. These experiments won't necessarily add to the body of scientific knowledge, but will give your child the opportunity to demonstrate how scientists prove their theories.

Photo by Sierra Weir

Mold Notebook for Science Project

In kindergarten, children work with questions such as "How much salt must be added to water to make an egg float?" or "Do plants grow better with or without light?" or, my personal favorite, "Does mold grow faster on bread with or without air?" (Due to concerns about allergies, students are generally no longer allowed to actually bring their moldy bread or other food to school. They must document their results with photographs.)

INDIVIDUAL ACADEMIC PROJECTS

Depending on the question that your child has decided to explore, he or she must next form a *hypothesis*. In other words, what does the experimentor (Susie) believe will be the results of her experiment? If Susie believes that plants will grow better with light, then she simply writes that statement as her hypothesis.

Next comes the interesting part. Susie must plant two identical seeds in two identical little glass jars using identical soil. She will then place those two pots in identical conditions, giving them the same amount of water, space, and heat. The only difference will be that one plant will be placed in the sun and one will be denied light. The presence or absence of light is called the *variable*. It is always preferable to plant the seed next to the edge of the jar so that the growth, even under the soil, can be observed. Susie will then patiently check her plants every 24 or 48 hours to see which of them grows fastest. Her log of events will reflect all of the materials she used and record her routine findings. She will learn to refer to her practices, observations, and documentation as her *methodology*.

Even though you already know which plant will grow fastest, you must allow your child to observe and record the results without your interference. Each day, you will witness your child's excitement as he or she actually learns through careful observation. At the end of the experiment (science projects generally have a one to three month lead time, depending on the grade level), you will assist your child in writing up her findings and conclusions. If she is lucky, she proves her hypothesis. But if she doesn't, it's still a valid science project and still a learning experience. Whether or not the hypothesis is proven, the student is usually asked how he or she could improve the project and whether any other experiments could be run based on the results of the project she did.

In some schools, demonstrations and surveys are also acceptable as science projects, even though they don't follow the scientific method. For example, if your child wants to demonstrate magnetic force, he or she can design one of those sailboats on a plastic tray, with magnets underneath that pull the boat around. Or do what my son and his dad did one year, demonstrate how pullies work by designing a contraption that lifts a can full of rocks.

CHAPTER TWO

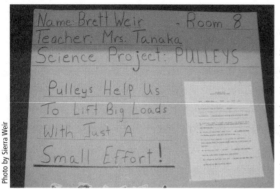

First Grade Level Science Project Display: How Pulleys Work, by Brett Weir

One year, a fifth-grade student conducted an experiment which showed which colors resulted when different metals were added to natural plant dyes. He used marigold petals and got various shades of yellow, gold, and a nearly green color. That experiment *definitely* required parental supervision, but was a tremendous learning experience for that student.

My daughter once did a rather sophisticated mold experiment in which we compared mold growth with and without air, but used four sets of four pairs of samples. The first week, we put two samples each of cheese, strawberries, bread, and lemon in eight separate containers. Four were sealed completely. She punched holes in the lids of the other four, which allowed air in. Each week for four weeks, we started another set. That way, my daughter was not only able to demonstrate whether the presence of air sped up or slowed down the mold process, she was able to show a four-week progression of mold on each of four foods. Of course, those were the days when we could still bring molding items into the school. However, I'm sure she could have documented her results with photos and shown equally impressive results.

You will be surprised at the level of sophistication that is demonstrated by middle school students in their selection and execution of science projects. By the time they are in sixth grade, they already have six years' worth of science projects under their belts. Many of them are, in a word, experts. They have fully absorbed the steps of the scientific method and are able to come up with new and intriguing ideas for exploration. Last year, my daughter's science experiment, "Does Having a Boyfriend or Girlfriend Affect Perception and Assessment of Attractiveness and Social Desirability?" (no kidding) took first place in her category (Behavioral Sciences) at her middle school.

INDIVIDUAL ACADEMIC PROJECTS

She went on to win second place at the County Science Fair, where she was required to stand in front of her project and defend its validity to a team of 3-4 judges. By the way, parents weren't allowed into the room where the judging was held. This is why teachers are teaching our children to stand up and talk in front of groups (see Chapter Four).

Photo by Kathie Weir

Los Angeles County Science Fair Winner, Sierra Weir, Nancy Bernstein's 8th Grade, Dodson Gifted and High Ability Magnet Middle School, RPV, CA

Creating a Great Project

1. **Start early**
2. **Choose a good topic**
3. **Take your time**
4. **Plan well**
5. **Complete your research**
6. **Make a colorful display**
7. **Give credit where credit is due**
8. **Think before you cut**
9. **Follow directions**
10. **Ask questions**
11. **Write a thorough paper**
12. **Meet your deadline**

During project set-up and after the judging, we were free to wander through the exhibition and view the competition. We were astonished to see some of the projects that middle school and high school students had developed and executed. Projects with names like "Fuel Cell Technology" and "Bridge Design" and "What Are the Parameters of Frictional Force?" or "It's Laughter I'm After" were all aesthetically assembled and flawlessly presented. Children who had already learned to take their work seriously and were able to successfully explain and defend it were awarded big prizes and the chance to go on to the state competition. These students are tomorrow's innovators. Projects which seemed to be of particular interest to the judges and which won the big-money corporation prizes involved innovations in recycling and technological advances, including fuel cells for electric cars and the "electronic nose" project. And to think it all starts with an egg in salt water!

CHAPTER TWO

State Project

By the time your child reaches fifth grade, he or she is being seriously prepped to succeed in middle school. It used to be that elementary schools lasted through sixth grade (perhaps some still do); frankly, I would prefer to give the kids an extra year in that sheltered elementary school environment. Unfortunately, the powers that be have decided otherwise. In fifth grade, teachers become more demanding, less coddling of your student. Names left off papers result in zeros. Teachers don't intend to punish the students; they simply want them to learn responsibility. Some of those lessons in responsibility come in the form of more complex and time-consuming projects. One of my favorites is the state project. Your child gets to pick the state he or she would like to learn more about, then do a multi-faceted report, complete with displays and oral presentations. This project usually lasts over a several-week period and can be lots of fun.

The first step involves having your child select a state to study. Then he or she writes, e-mails, or phones the State Department of Tourism and requests a packet of information. Start early on this one, because it can take up to two weeks to get the information. In the meantime, have your child plot out the main tasks of the assignment on a calendar, along with an estimated time to complete each task. Our state project was worth a total of 250 points. The teacher provided a list of sub-tasks, each of which was worth 5-25 points. For example, the student has to draw or illustrate the state flag, state flower, and state bird. Some teachers only allow hand drawings; others will accept computer graphics or downloaded photos. Another part of the assignment involved drawing two state maps, one showing topography and one showing products.

My daughter's fifth grade teacher also required a 2-5 page report, in which the student was required to include information regarding the state's history, population, famous people, major products and industries, size, bordering states, natural resources, educational facilities, type of government, and other pertinent facts. Each student also delivered an oral report summarizing the main points of interest about his state. My son's teacher required that the students research all the same areas, but they were only required to take notes and deliver the oral report; no written report was required.

INDIVIDUAL ACADEMIC PROJECTS

Photo by Sierra Weir

Indiana State Project by Sierra Weir

Photo by Sierra Weir

Montana State Project by Brett Weir

Finally, the student was required to develop a model or display which thoroughly described the state and its most important features. This was the child's opportunity to be creative and informative. My daughter, who reported on Indiana, developed a set of laminated cards, "Indiana A-Z," which she displayed in a CD rack. My son prepared a three-way display board complete with photos he had taken himself, magazine illustrations, and maps. He also made up a small display of arrowheads, mineral samples, and other artifacts from his chosen state, Montana. Both kids had a lot of fun and became experts on a state other than California.

CHAPTER TWO

Rockets

The rocket project is an interesting cross between an individual and a group project. Each child in the class is responsible to build and paint a rocket (from a kit). This draws upon their artistic skills – no two rockets ever turn out alike – as it teaches them the scientific principles of aerodynamics and physics. As the rockets reach completion, they are lined up around the classroom, lending a colorful background to the learning environment.

Rockets ready to go, by students in Bruce Dalrymple's 5th Grade, White Point School, San Pedro, CA

Rocket Launch

Rockets are usually launched in late spring. The teacher keeps a close eye on the weather, waiting for the exact conditions that will promote the launch: clear, warm, with not a hint of breeze in the air. A huge contraption is pulled out onto the playground and several rockets are loaded on at once. The launch is closely supervised and carefully planned. On launch days, excited parents and teachers gather on the playground to see how far the rockets go. Later, students measure angles to determine which rockets achieved the greatest height and distance.

INDIVIDUAL ACADEMIC PROJECTS

Stock Market Analysis

Another fifth grade project that helps children extend their conceptualization of statistics and percentages is one in which the child picks three or four stocks from the newspaper, then follows their ups and downs over a 4-6 week period. This project gives the child an introduction to the stock market and how values of stocks can change on a daily basis. It is fairly simple for the child to show the stock movements with a drawing or via computer graphics.

Stock Portfolio, Sierra Weir, from Gayle Whitsett's 5th Grade, White Point School, San Pedro, CA

Vertebrate and Invertebrate Notebooks

In fifth grade, my daughter was responsible for compiling two rather long reports: one on vertebrates and the other on invertebrates. She was required to write one paragraph about each of ten types of vertebrates and invertebrates, then draw the creature that she had discussed. Though this project elicited many tears (I *can't* draw this!!), it resulted in a pair of fairly accomplished notebooks that I personally felt were a seventh-grade level project. Remember, fifth

grade is about getting the kids ready for middle school. After those reports were completed, I never again heard my daughter complain about not being able to draw. Completing that project gave her a confidence about her ability to do whatever it took to meet the project requirements.

Vertebrates and Invertebrates Notebooks, by Sierra Weir, from Gayle Whitsett's class.

CHAPTER TWO

History and Geography

6th Grade Newspaper Project (left), Hieroglyphics and Sarcophogas (right) by Brett Weir. Social Studies projects from Kevin Allen's 6th Grade Social Studies class, Dodson Gifted & High Ability Magnet Middle School, RPV, CA

If I had to choose the type of projects I like to see my children bring home, I would have to say history and geography projects are among my favorites. These days, teachers are coming up with some really interesting ways to make history come alive for their students.

In sixth grade, my son studied Ancient Egypt, China, Rome, and Greece. His projects included everything from a hieroglyphics notebook to a postcard from China to a travel brochure for Ancient Egypt. They also studied maps and completed a globe project. In seventh grade, he wrote papers on the Five Pillars of Islam, the ancient Kongo Kingdom of Africa, and Caligula. He also constructed a model of an Egyptian sarcophagus and a Greek vase, two detailed maps, and model dwellings of ancient peoples.

Maps (above) and Globes, Laura Freeman's 6th Grade Social Studies class, Dodson Gifted & High Ability Magnet Middle School, RPV, CA

INDIVIDUAL ACADEMIC PROJECTS

Dioramas

The first time you hear of this assignment, you might be like me and ask, "a dio – what?" Dioramas resemble little stage scenes; they are prepared as if inside a box, with the box turned on its side and the open end toward the audience. Inside the box, the child creates a little world that reflects a literary or historical or dramatic event. Dioramas are usually not very large, about two by two feet maximum. I have seen some that are one foot by one foot by one foot, which challenge the student's ability to miniaturize his scene. Dioramas are often used by teachers in connection with book reports. Your child may be asked to show his favorite scene in three dimensions. Here is where your child can make use of items that you have been saving: old pieces of foam, Styrofoam, cardboard shapes, tiny plastic figures, corks, and fabric scraps. It's a bit like furnishing a dollhouse, though I would advise that you never mention that to your middle school student!

"What A Soldier Carried With Him" Diorama by Sierra Weir

I recently saw an interesting diorama that a child had constructed to use as a stage for a puppet show. The floor was a piece of plywood and the stage curtains were set up on PVC pipe. There was a partition in the middle of the floor, with different sets painted on either side, so that they could change scenes. The puppets were manipulated from the side of the stage. It was a simple, but a very effective design.

CHAPTER TWO

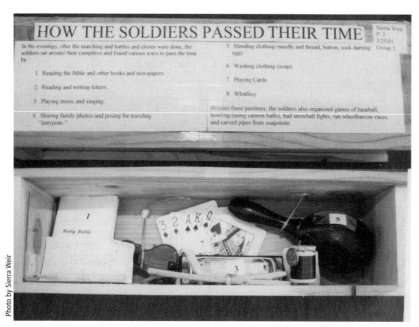

"How The Soldiers Passed Their Time" Diorama by Sierra Weir

Sometimes, the teacher will assign a diorama project in connection with a "describing yourself" type of project. In other words, the child will be asked to arrange a certain number of items in the box that define the child's past, present, or future. Or the assignment might involve creating a scene or scenes that reflect the child's family, favorite pastimes, or most recent vacation. Dioramas can also depict scientific concepts or nature scenes. They often have moving or pop-up parts that can be controlled from behind the back wall of the box. The last one we did showed Nancy Drew stuck in a well that was mysteriously located under a barn. Unfortunately, that one never made it home from school.

Chapter Three

Group Projects

Why Group Projects?

A classroom is more than a group of students and a teacher. It is also a community of people who must share the same working and learning space for six hours a day in elementary school and one hour a day in middle school (which can seem like six hours if the "community" is not working together). Based on my own experience and the reports of teachers whom I have either worked with or talked to, a teacher's primary concern is keeping order in her classroom. If there is no order, the teacher wastes most of his or her time trying to control or contain the disorderly elements of the classroom.

CHAPTER THREE

Teachers do their best to figure out the most workable seating arrangement (often changing seats to place more compatible children near one another or regularly rotating seating arrangements in order to encourage more interaction among diverging groups or individuals). They institute systems of reward and consequences that encourage good behavior and sometimes arrange desks in "teams" and "pods" whose behavior and achievements are counted toward group rewards. The assignment of group projects is yet another way that teachers have to bring disparate individuals together in an educational setting. Sometimes, a shared goal will help two or three otherwise unlikely comrades find a way to coexist. At the very least, a group project changes the dynamics of the classroom for a certain time period.

It has always been obvious to me that teachers who assign group projects are doing so based on a vision of a future shared world that our children will inhabit together. I think their intentions are good. Teachers who are successful in creating a true team mentality in their classrooms are able to give the children a much more positive educational experience. I have had the pleasure of substitute teaching in classes where everything came together and the students acted as a unit in achieving their own educational goals. I have also been in classes where three or four disruptive children have consistently ruined things for the other fifteen or twenty children.

A teacher may use her tested and successful methods of classroom management on one class and have an excellent and productive year, then use the exact same methods the next year, with disastrous results. Instead of running from these difficult situations, most teachers seek out or develop new approaches to education. Group projects, including grouping children to work in rotating groups for short time intervals, seem to give students a slightly different perspective on the learning process and provide a successful management technique for teachers.

Whether group projects help or hurt the classroom environment depends on the teacher, that year's classroom mix, the parents, and the kids. I understand why teachers assign them and I even support their reasons for doing so. In this chapter, I will try to help you understand how to guide your children through group projects with a minimum of distress.

GROUP PROJECTS

Problems with Group Projects

I won't lie; I am not a big fan of group projects in elementary or middle schools. In fact, I am not a great fan of group projects in any walk of life, including jobs, unless there is a definite leader who assigns tasks to group members. As I have assisted my children through their many projects, I have discussed my viewpoint with various teachers, most of whom explained their reasons for utilizing group projects.

My reasons for not liking group projects can be summed up in a few sentences; most children, right up through high school age, are not mature enough to cooperate equitably in doing the work of a group project. Therefore, one of two things usually happens; within the group of four to six children, there is a battle for leadership, usually based on popularity. This is often followed by a definite shutting out of the unpopular one or two kids in the group. The other three or four children then either proceed to do some or all of the project, while complaining that the other two aren't helping. Second scenario: the two outcasts do an entire project on their own, then bring it to school as the "group project." Only problem, the other four already produced a "group project" and aren't willing to include the others' work. Third alternative: on the day the project is due, there are five or six kids scurrying around trying to make one cohesive project out of two or more uncoordinated sections or blaming each other for not getting it done on time or correctly.

I can't tell you how many times I have witnessed a little knot of boys or girls outside the classroom on the day the project is due, pointing fingers and calling each other names because someone forgot to call someone, type something, or bring something. The lines of dissension are almost always clearly defined based on who walks home from school with whom, who plays or eats lunch with whom, and/or those who regularly earn better grades versus those who earn lesser grades. This may come as a surprise, but most kids don't want to "tattle" to the teacher in this situation. And, to be fair, teachers sometimes tell the students that handling such power struggles is part of the project. The only reasonable solution is parental guidance and intervention.

CHAPTER THREE

Teachers assign projects for a variety of reasons, but the one I have heard most often in regard to group projects is that it advances the child's group dynamics skills. In other words, it is a form of social engineering, preparing the child for future careers in which he or she will have to work in group settings to produce a proposal, then build that proposal into a manufactured item or system. All well and good, except that the rather competitive environment in which our children are otherwise being educated doesn't lend itself to cooperation, especially where a group grade is involved. Most children are dealing with enough pressures both in- and outside of schools without being expected to exercise adaptive counseling skills in the sixth or seventh grade.

Teachers usually have a more optimistic view of the purpose of group projects. They see them as helping the group to bond, allowing kids who would otherwise not speak to one another the opportunity to learn of each other's strengths, and to provide a flowering of the "group dynamic" within each young student. One teacher recently told me that she believes a group project must have a "leader" if it is to work. She believes that children will naturally develop a method of choosing a leader as part of the group project dynamic. I have often seen the opposite, with group projects destroying former friendships or causing a definite hardening of formerly held group boundaries. One thing I really dread seeing is when the teacher decides to boost the social life of several "outsider" type kids by assigning them all to the same group. Just because a kid is on the outside doesn't mean he wants to join an outsiders' group.

If a group project is going to be run entirely in school, that is one thing. As long as the teacher allows everyone time to complete it and monitors the in-fighting, the project can be successful. However, if the teacher expects the kids to work together on the project outside of school, things can get complicated. This problem is particularly daunting in city schools, where everyone doesn't live around the block or neighborhood. And this is where parents have no choice but to engineer, communicate, and participate. Either that, or let your child do the whole project alone, which, believe me, has happened in our home.

GROUP PROJECTS

Communication, Coordination, Cooperation: Helping Your Child Manage a Group Project

Through trial and error (sometimes HUGE error), I have learned that there are three simple steps that parents can and must take to ensure that their student's group project at least has a shot at success. All three come under what I call the "Three C's": communication, coordination, and cooperation.

I usually get my first hint about a pending group project when I see my son or daughter come out of school with a certain disgusted look on his or her face. I brace myself and ask the standard, "So, how was school today?" and am greeted with a blast of irritation. "We got another stupid group project. And I hate my group. I'm in with Jimmy again, the same one that did nothing on the social studies project," etc. I take a deep breath and steel myself for the inevitable group project dilemmas.

Communication

As with individual projects, always start by asking your child to produce the written assignment. Discuss it thoroughly, then have your child talk to the teacher to clear up any misunderstood terms, tasks, or duties. The most important question to ask is whether the project will be conducted inside or outside of school or both. If the teacher says that it is an in-school project, that usually means that certain class periods will be devoted to letting the children do library or Internet research in school. Your child may still have to make a poster or edit everyone's written contributions into one paper that has to be typed, or gather other materials outside of school, but you may not have to arrange or sponsor any out-of-school meetings for the group.

My daughter was recently assigned a project that involved four students making one poster. They divided up the poster into four parts that will be joined at school. I personally think this is a bad idea because it may look like exactly that: four different posters taped together. But she is having a difficult time getting her three project mates (all boys) to agree to an out-of-school meeting time and place. I told her to just pretend she's the boss

CHAPTER THREE

and write up assignments. She's already decided that the boys have to turn their work in to *her* at least three days before the teacher gets it, so that she will have the weekend to "fix it up." This may sound harsh, but she's had several bad experiences with group projects (including a misunderstanding where everyone did the same part of the assignment and no one did the other two parts). Since the teacher is giving everyone the same grade, she intends to cover all bases.

If the teacher expects some out-of-school effort by individuals that will be coordinated by the group outside of school, you will probably have to help your child in the communication department. Communication can be accomplished via e-mail or telephone. In this most recent group project, my daughter would rather do the entire project herself than have to call a boy at home. I had to threaten and cajole and coax her to make those calls. Then, of course, only one boy even bothered to answer her call. They're fourteen years old. They have better things to do than coordinate a school event.

That brings up another problem with group projects; often, everyone in the group gets the same grade, regardless of who did what. This is where our competitive cultural approach is nothing more than a hindrance to the group's well-being. Some children will go all out to get that grade; it's in their natures. The others will sit back and do nothing, then get the same grade. We are all familiar with this scenario in college and in the workplace. Reference my opposition to group projects.

To be fair, some teachers have assured me that the child's grade is mostly a result of the child's individual effort and that the group project model is simply for purposes of teaching the child to function in a group. One very resourceful teacher even showed me her "peer evaluation sheet" which she hands out after a group project. Each child fills out the form to indicate how much time and effort each student contributed to the project. She then uses the whole group's forms in conjunction with her own evaluation of their individual and group effort to come up with a grade.

GROUP PROJECTS

Name:_____

Per._____

Group Names	Responsibility	% Effort

Use the table above to rate the amount of effort each member of your group has put into this project, then create a pie graph showing each persons effort towards the final project.

Peer Evaluation Sheet for Group Projects by Teresa L. Baumann, 8th Grade Social Studies teacher, Dodson Gifted & High Ability Magnet Middle School, RPV, CA

You will be responsible to model the behaviors that you hope your child will learn from participating in a group project. I always encourage my child to become the defacto group leader by contacting everyone as soon as the project is assigned. If he or she is unable to coordinate a meeting date or time, or if the outside work involves going someplace, e.g., a museum or library, then I take over the phone calling and scheduling through the parents. If we still can't muster any cooperation, we take the issue to the teacher.

Another problem that often surfaces with group projects is that teachers sometimes seem oblivious of social groupings. Assigning a group of kids to pull their chairs together in the classroom and work cooperatively on a project is vastly different from assigning an outside-of-school project with the expectation that a certain little clique of girls will include the other two girls who are seen as social undesirables. I have seen group projects go down the tubes because half the group didn't want to be seen with the other half in the library or because none of the kids felt comfortable even *talking* to the others outside of school. This gets even further complicated when boys and girls are assigned to projects together in middle school. Parents have no choice but to take the lead!

CHAPTER THREE

Group Project Checklist

Communicate!
1. You talk to your child.
2. Your child talks to the teacher.
3. Your child talks to his group members.
4. You talk to other parents.
5. You talk to the teacher.

Coordinate!
1. Group agrees on assigned tasks.
2. Group arranges meetings.
3. Group meets deadlines.

Cooperate!
1. Stay in touch.
2. Discuss sources and problems.
3. Share materials.
4. Offer rides.
5. Suggest field trips.

Coordinating Meetings and Tasks

First, get over your own fear of calling people whom you have never met and with whom you may have nothing in common. You will be surprised how often your phone call is the first time that the other kids' parents have heard about the project. Sometimes, the parent tells you he or she needs to talk to their child, then get back to you. I have found that, although most parents really want to help, they either don't know how or feel they don't have the time. You can be more effective by helping your child analyze the project before you make the calls, so that you have an idea of what needs to be done.

Be thankful if your child lives in the same general area as the rest of her group members. We have had situations where two of the group members lived over an hour away and whose families would have had to rely on public transportation for weekend meetings. Those children were thus precluded from some of the background work that the other children did (e.g., trips to a local museum for photos and docent information sessions). The other group members felt cheated and put upon, but the problem just wasn't fixable.

Make sure that you ask whether each child has access to a computer to type up his or her section of the project. If not, perhaps one child can take charge of typing up the others' handwritten work. One thing your child should avoid is handing in a project that is four-fifths neatly typed and one-fifth scrawled on notebook paper. Teachers tend to take for granted that one or more children have computers available or parents willing to take them to the library or Kinko's, where they might use one. But we have learned the hard way that this is not always true. In the last referenced project, the children who couldn't make it to the meetings also lacked access to computers. My daughter ended up typing their handwritten contributions. More complaints.

GROUP PROJECTS

Cooperate

If you can find the time after school or on weekends, encourage your child to offer your home as headquarters for the project. If they haven't already done so in school, have the students hold a preliminary meeting to brainstorm the plan. Encourage them to divide up the tasks and prepare a workable schedule. Organize carpools to take your child's group to museums, libraries, or related events that will enhance their understanding of their project. Watching an educational video at home might also help.

Be aware that most parents are not going to be as eager to help as you would like them to be. For a variety of reasons, including work and other family obligations, they will not come through for the group. Other parents simply refuse to "do my kid's homework." I have learned to be happy if the other parents simply produce their kids to work on the project at the right times and places. The main issue is that the kids learn to analyze and interpret the assignment, then produce a project that meets the requirements. To the extent possible, I stay out of the decision-making, acting as more of a behind-the-scenes assistant and chauffeur. Well, okay, I am also the first one to run out and make sure they have all the necessary materials, and I might offer a word or two of advice.

What to Expect

The main difference between individual and group projects is that the former is done by an individual whereas the latter represents a joint effort. Sometimes, teachers assign either/or projects. Students can do the assignment alone or with one or more other people. If the assignment includes, say, a three-page paper and a display, she will require each child to produce the three-page paper, but they may cooperate on a display. All of the projects mentioned in Chapter Two could conceivably be assigned as group projects.

Be careful of what I call "coat-tail kids," i.e., students who know that your child does excellent work and always ask to make individual projects into "group projects" with your child or always seeks to work with your child in groups. Sometimes, kids are just taking advantage. If your child seems to be always doing an inordinate amount of work and is always working with the

CHAPTER THREE

same set of students, then you should contact the teacher and discuss the issue. I doubt any teacher wants a student to be taken advantage of. I also doubt that your child wants the burden of drawing attention to herself over such an issue. You may have to contact the teacher privately (don't even tell your kid) and let her know what you have observed.

I am always in favor of helping other students who work with my child, particularly if that child seems to be disadvantaged in terms of getting support or assistance from his parents. However, I do require that the other kids put in some effort on a project, even if my daughter is willing to "do it all" just to avoid an argument. I model the art of speaking up for oneself and the value of communication as a tool to defuse most problems. In life, your child will have to face many of the same situations and people that she must deal with in school. Teach her to demand equity in all situations, including school projects.

On the bright side, many group projects do seem to work out well. At the county and state level science fairs, you will see many projects on which students successfully cooperated. We want our children to become competent at working in groups of all types. School is a good place to start that process.

Sample Group Projects

Most elementary school group projects will be completed in school. They may include doing in-class reports and dramatizations of assigned books, science units, and illustrated stories on the computer. Even in the lower grades, students begin to see the strengths of others based on their joint work. My son is an excellent artist. By second grade, he was routinely being asked to do all the illustrations for a project, which he thoroughly enjoyed. In third grade, my daughter complained that, in her science experiment group, the boys did all the fun stuff and only let the girls take notes and write up the reports. Trust me, that practice ended as soon as she told me about it.

GROUP PROJECTS

Primary Grade Group Projects

The Apple Project

Many early group projects are group projects merely by virtue of the fact that the kids are divided into groups in the classroom to do them. Parents are usually involved as classroom helpers. One of my favorites from kindergarten was when the kids did their "Apple Project." Every child was asked to bring in an apple. The first part of the project involved lining all twenty apples up to see how many different kinds of apples there are. (Usually, the teacher also brings in a few apples, in case the kids happen to all bring in the same variety.)

Next, the kids were divided into groups. Each group was given a large sheet of white construction paper and smaller squares of construction paper in various shades of red and green. There were also several magazines and food newspaper advertisements on each table, from which they could cut pictures of apples, moms, dads, kids, apple pie, apple sauce, etc.

The classroom helper (usually a mom) wrote a capital "A" and "apple" at the top of the large sheet. Students were instructed to draw and cut out several apples from the colored paper to paste on their white sheet. Then they were allowed to cut out apple-related items from the newspaper and magazines to make an apple collage. The result: five beautiful "group-constructed" apple collages.

The last part of the apple project was the most fun. The teacher had brought in a blender. Classroom helpers were asked to peel and core the apples and cut them into small chunks. The teacher added a little sugar to the apples, then blended them into fresh homemade applesauce. This is an interdisciplinary project because it involves art, spelling, following directions, working together, identifying appropriate photos, learning about different varieties of apples, and cooking. The kids just thought they were having fun. Use pumpkins or squash and you could change it to a party activity for Halloween or Thanksgiving (except you'd have to make the pies or pumpkin seeds ahead of time).

CHAPTER THREE

Letter Pretzels

Just make sure all the kids wash their hands before and after touching food of any kind. Also, you'll need lots of class helpers to keep the kids safe around the toaster oven or when cutting apples. Depending on the school district, you may actually have to go to the cafeteria to do the cutting or baking part. There are some strict "zero tolerance" rules in place in many areas. Always check with the teacher and principal before you decide to conduct any project in the classroom.

> This is another easy letter recognition/cooking lesson, which can be done by small in-class groups using a toaster oven:
>
> 1. Dissolve one tablespoon of yeast in 1/2 cup of warm water.
> 2. Add one teaspoon of honey and one teaspoon of salt.
> 3. Add 1-1/3 cup of flour.
> 4. Knead well.
> 5. Roll pieces into long strips. Form letters on wax paper, using a letter guide.
> 6. Brush with beaten egg.
> 7. Sprinkle with salt (coarse salt if available).
> 8. Bake for 10 minutes at 425 degrees.
> 9. Cool before eating.

Fourth and Fifth Grade Group Projects

Birth of a Star Project

My son recalls the "Birth of a Star Project" well. Each group was asked to illustrate and explain a different stage in the birth of a star. As usual, he was asked to illustrate. He finished his illustrations one day, then was out sick the next day. When he came back, he discovered that his group had decided to color his drawing. To put it mildly, he was a bit perturbed. This was his "I only do black-and-white drawings" stage. It took the teacher a little while to smooth that one over. At the end of the project, the teacher hung the various stages of the star in order for a classroom display.

Book Characters Puppet Show

One of the less stressful fourth grade projects I have heard about was called the "Book Characters Puppet Show." The class was divided into six groups of either five or six children. Each group was assigned a different book to read in class. Each student then selected one or more characters and made a puppet to represent that character.

GROUP PROJECTS

The students chose one or two favorite chapters in the book, then adapted that section to a play. The children each had to learn their character's lines. The mom who told me about this project said that the children were able to do most of their work in school or individually at home (e.g., learning lines and making the puppets). They did have to get together two or three times over a two-week period to run through their skit.

For that project, students were graded individually for their puppets and their memorization, but 30% of their grade was based on the jointly written and acted play. The project was such a success that the students ended up acting their skits out on stage at an assembly for the entire school.

Middle School Projects

My children have been in middle school for the past two-three years. I don't know if it is just California or if projects are this popular everywhere, but from September to June, we seem to barely finish one before another starts up. For some reason, I feel competent to cope with the individual projects, even when they seem to piggyback one another with incredible regularity. It's the group projects that keep us all on edge.

Roman History

Both my son's and daughter's sixth grade classes devoted considerable time to the Romans. My daughter's school sponsored a "Roman Days" event, wherein a professional educational acting group came into the school and organized a Roman cultural setting. They wore togas and played games and ate Roman food. The group part of that unit involved the students being divided into teams that competed against one another both at the main event and for a couple of weeks prior.

Each team was assigned a different aspect of Roman history or culture on which to report. Within the team, each member was given a sub-assignment. My daughter, who was assigned to be Nero, researched Roman government. On her team's day, she had to turn in her written report, make a five-minute presentation about her subject, then give a five-question quiz to her class-

CHAPTER THREE

mates. Her presentation was judged based on how well she presented the material *and* on how well the other students did on her quiz. In other words, was she interesting enough to hold their attention and did she give a clear enough presentation that they were able to recall her key points?

Though I struggled with making the toga, I liked the Roman Days event because I could see that the kids enjoyed it. Giving each child an opportunity to express him or herself in writing, to quiz the other kids, to dress up, and to win prizes, was a great way to emphasize the material and make it real to them. At the end of the event, the teams were awarded medals according to their total point scores.

Greek Days, a similar event sponsored by my son's sixth grade, is discussed under "Schoolwide Projects," pg. 110.

Seventh Grade China News Project

In seventh grade, my son's first history group project involved producing a "news show" as if it were presented in Six Dynasties China. They named the TV station China Broadcasting System (CBS). Each student was assigned to do a segment of the news, as it is done today: latest events, weather, sports, entertainment, war, religion, art, archeology, and human interest were all included. Each child wrote a section or two.

Besides being responsible for his own section, my son volunteered to type up the final product, no small job, considering he also had to keep it within a newscaster format, changing names and inserting anchor and reporter small talk where required. When the report was fully written, they recorded it on video as if it were a news report. Very creative.

I particularly liked that report because the teacher was wise enough to let them do most of it during class time. My son went to the library and researched the Internet from home, but we didn't have to organize any outside-of-school meetings, so it went a lot more smoothly than some group projects.

GROUP PROJECTS

Eighth Grade Civil War Project

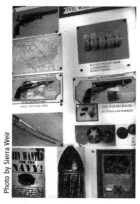

Photo by Sierra Weir

Civil War Weapons Poster
by Sierra Weir

In eighth grade, students are introduced to the Civil War in all its amazing and horrifying detail. My daughter's class was assigned to do a group project that spanned about six weeks. Each group was told to research a particular area of the war, such as medicine, battlefields, transportation, food and clothing, political climate, etc. My daughter's group researched battlefields. The group decided on how to focus that topic.

The group consisted of five students, two of whom lived too far away to get together with the other three on weekends, so the onus of the project fell on those three students. Fortunately, all three sets of parents were equally motivated to assist their children. At first, the kids decided to bring in some Civil War era guns that belonged to one of the student's gun collector cousins. The principal said that would be fine, as long as the gun barrels were filled with cement. Needless to say, that idea fell by the wayside.

Having been raised on the East Coast myself, it never occurred to me that California had any involvement in the Civil War. I was astonished to learn that California not only was involved in the Civil War, but that the Union Army Headquarters for Southern California and the Arizona Territory from 1861-1871 is located within five miles of our home. The parents organized a trip for the kids to see the Drum Barracks Civil War Museum, housed in the last remaining wooden building of Camp Drum. There, they were able to observe a fascinating display of period furniture, clothing, army gear, and weapons (including a full-size original Gatling gun) as they appeared in the Civil War era. That evening, they rented and watched one of the better Civil War movie series.

For her part of the project, my daughter used two wine boxes with plexiglass fronts to construct two miniature museum type displays of items that Civil War soldiers carried with them and used to entertain themselves. We were able to find most of the items around our house or in the home of her grandparents.

CHAPTER THREE

She also studied the list of Civil War soldiers' rations and made a small display showing the types of food they were given by the Union Army. The group also designed two posters of battlefields and weapons used in those battles. Despite the inability of two group members to fully participate, this was one of the more successful group projects in which either of my children has been involved.

Bank Project

Photo by Sierra Weir

Dodson Federal is located in Matt Sprenger's 6th Grade Classroom at Dodson Middle School, RPV, CA

One of the sixth grade math and science teachers who responded to my survey wrote about an interesting ongoing group project that he created and which he conducts in his classroom throughout the year. The purpose of the "Bank Project" is twofold: one, it sets up a very creative reward and consequence system whereby students are actually "paid" for completing their in-class work. They then are able to set up bank accounts at "Dodson Federal," an actual mini-bank built in the back of the classroom.

The children are taught to operate the bank. They learn about keeping track of their customer accounts, the purpose of interest, and how to keep and balance a checkbook or fill out a deposit slip. You can imagine what a boost this is to their math skills and their understanding of money concepts, something we all want our children to know.

Photo by Sierra Weir

Cash and Deposit Slips from Dodson Federal

Secondly, the children have an incentive to complete their classroom work. Mr. Sprenger runs a store, where children can use their earned income to purchase items. The beauty of this system is that it adds a dimension of real life to the classroom. Students are given an incentive to participate (cash payments) and rewards (purchase of items), while simultaneously learning some of the more complex workings of our economic and banking system. Bravo to teachers who are willing to get creative to teach our children!

Chapter Four

Presentations and Demonstrations

Not Just "Show and Tell" Anymore

Remember grade school "Show and Tell," where you'd bring something from home, your favorite toy, a special photo, or even a pet, and then spend three minutes in front of the class talking about it? In second grade, I remember struggling to choose between my collection of plastic charms (which my mother didn't want me to bring because she was afraid I would lose them) and the yellow rabbit's foot that I got for my birthday from my best friend. Since I was attending a Catholic school at the time, I was also allowed to bring religious items, including pictures of saints, a hand-made set of rosary beads that belonged to my grandmother, and a velvet cover for my child-size prayer book. Those were the days. Some kids never brought a thing and some, like me, had something to show or tell nearly every day. Big surprise that I turned out to be a writer.

CHAPTER FOUR

Fast forward to today's schools, where "show and tell" still exists in nearly its original form, but only in early primary years, i.e., kindergarten and first grades, and sometimes into second grade. Kids are still allowed to bring personal and non-school related items to participate in "Share Time." I've even seen pets in school in the lower grades, but, due to fears of lawsuits over allergies or injuries, permission to bring any type of animal on campus, including performing mice for science projects, is fast becoming history.

Because teachers are busy and administrations wish to discourage kids from bringing toys to school, many teachers now request that all show and tell or share items have some educational relevance. In other words, they like to see the children bring books, photos, or scientific items (e.g., arrowheads, mineral and rock samples, craft items that they made or helped make), antiques or historical documents, etc. Teachers generally don't want to see balloons, water guns (or *any* type of gun), messy items, toys (even educational toys) with lots of small pieces, inappropriate items, photos, or music, or anything that is too large or fragile for the child to handle (unless Mom is there to help). Remember, the teacher only has a few minutes each day to devote to these peripheral activities, which are mostly intended to make the child feel comfortable and encourage a "getting-to-know-you" atmosphere in the classroom. Help the teacher by steering your child away from bringing items that will cause too much excitement or chaos in the classroom.

Photo by Kathie Weir

Gathering Shells for a Presentation

PRESENTATIONS & DEMONSTRATIONS

What Is a Presentation?

A presentation usually involves one or more children who have prepared specific information to present to the class. A child may be expected to present an assignment or small project to the class in the form of giving a short description of it (e.g., a science project), reading it (e.g., a poem or story), performing a skit or musical act, or leading the class discussion regarding an assigned part of the text or lesson plan. Presentations differ from projects in that they are usually not as time intensive. The teacher will usually assign a simple presentation with a shorter deadline. If the presentation is part of a larger project, the teacher will make the students aware of that fact.

Within the classroom setting, teachers seek to give students various opportunities to experience what it is like to stand in front of the class. In this way, students become accustomed to being the center of attention and to thinking on their feet. For many students, this is the "I'd-rather-die-than-stand-up-there" experience. They are terrified. Particularly in middle school, where fellow students can be merciless, it is extremely difficult for children to stand before their peers and speak with confidence. All the more reason to do it! Assuming that most of our children will someday attend college, hold down good jobs, and participate in social events, we should do everything possible to help them get over their fear of public speaking.

Photo by Sierra Weir

Presentation of Original Poetry

Within the academic realm alone, various situations will arise where your child must be willing to address the class and make sense when he talks. Some examples include spelling bees; interviews for private schools and college (often with more than one interviewer present); school assemblies; running for school offices; participation in school plays; explaining science projects to teams of judges; and participating in talent shows. In middle school, my daughter and her classmates were each assigned to "teach" certain units of their social studies textbooks. That meant they really had to review the materials and be able to answer other students' questions about their designated sections. Everyone got a turn, so it was fair.

CHAPTER FOUR

What Is a Demonstration?

A demonstration resembles a presentation, but often involves the use of props. These days, teachers tend to do everything possible to help kids get extra credit. One of the most common things I have observed is the "Give a Demonstration" opportunity. The students are told that they can conduct a demonstration for the class in any area where they feel they have expertise. It goes without saying that such demonstrations have to be approved by the teacher. Demonstrations generally don't require much preparation because the student already has (or should have) a knowledge of his subject. Therefore, there are usually much shorter deadlines. Also, demonstrations are often voluntary. Perhaps only 20-30% of the class will participate.

When my daughter was in third grade, she taught herself to do Origami, the Japanese art of folding paper into interesting shapes and containers. From

that point forward, through about seventh or eighth grade, her demonstration involved Origami. She would take in enough pieces of Origami paper to give each student two sheets. Then she would teach the class how to create one or two different simple animals or objects. For a finale, she would demonstrate a really difficult sequence of folding that resulted in a more sophisticated model.

Photo by Sierra Weir

Materials for Origami Demonstration

PRESENTATIONS & DEMONSTRATIONS

Some students perform simple cooking demonstrations. They bring the ingredients and show how they would be mixed together. Instead of actually trying to cook in the room, they bring in samples of the finished dish and let people taste it. My daughter got her first taste of California sushi roll this way and has been making and eating them ever since. Several children prepared Jello and one baked a German chocolate cake. The issue is clearly not the level of skill required to perform the activity; it is the child's willingness to get up there and, in effect, lead the class.

If there is enough space available, students may demonstrate dance steps or gymnastics moves. One student showed how to plant seeds, then handed out directions he had researched for planting seasonal gardens (see the end of this chapter for details). My daughter once took a tour of her grandparents' house and gathered up a selection of historical items from their collection of antiques. In class, she discussed how things were done "back then" versus "now."

Photo by Sierra Weir

Antique household items used in history demonstration: mortar and pestle; 17th Century Danish beeswax candle and bronze candleholder; 19th Century vegetable chopper and wooden bowl.

Another showed the many uses of pumpkins by carving a jack-o-lantern, demonstrating how to dry pumpkin seeds, and then reviewing the steps to make pumpkin pie. He also brought in five or six homemade pies and gave each student a small piece. Lots of extra credit for that one!

CHAPTER FOUR

How You Can Help

The most important things you can do to help your child be prepared for various types of presentations and demonstrations is to be aware of what is going on in your child's academic life. As discussed throughout this book, that means asking questions, staying in close contact with the teacher, and being involved in your child's homework. There is nothing more frustrating than to have your child tell you about a really neat idea he has for a demonstration that is due tomorrow. Had you only known, you would have been more than willing to help him prepare for it. But now it is too late.

Presentations usually require at least a prepared talk of some kind. Teachers advise students to outline their thoughts on a set of index cards. They don't necessarily want the student to write an essay on the cards or read it to the class. Each card should include one of the main ideas or topics he is planning to discuss.

For example, if he is giving a talk on how to keep your pet healthy, he should have one card with key words about bathing your dog regularly, how often, where, and what pet shampoo he recommends. The next card might give a few hints about doggie exercise, walking the dog, making sure he has enough space in the yard, giving him toys.

Another card may deal with how to take care of your dog when she is about to have puppies and how to care for and find homes for puppies. A fourth card might give a rundown on the best types of dogs to own if you have kids or cats in the house. The cards should merely prompt your child to speak extemporaneously on his subject.

Your child can practice his presentation by standing in front of you and going through his talk a few times. You can coach him on standing up straight, making eye contact with the audience, and speaking slowly and clearly. Drill him on avoiding the use of "filler" words such as "umm, uh, like, you know," etc. Ask him several questions to prepare him for the most likely questions the other students will ask.

PRESENTATIONS & DEMONSTRATIONS

Visual Aids for Presentations

If your child is giving a five-minute presentation about dogs, it will probably help for him to assemble a "visual aid" about dogs, dog washing, dog raising, dog food, etc. A visual aid can be a small poster or flyer that enhances or reinforces the content of your child's presentation. In the above example, it could be a poster showing various breeds of dogs, a selection of dog toys and products, or a small stuffed dog and plastic container to show how to properly bathe a dog. Assembling such a poster shouldn't take much time; your child could either access a dog enthusiasts' website and download pictures, find photos from your family album, or browse a few magazines to get all the visuals he needs. Then he would add a few headings and captions to emphasize the main points of his talk. If the poster isn't free-standing, he could prop it up on the chalk tray of the blackboard for ease of referral.

If your child opts for a flyer instead, it's probably best to stick to a black-and-white presentation, because color printing and copies can be costly. He would probably include a few images, perhaps a chart or two about the relative sizes of dogs and how much they would cost to feed, and the names and addresses of local pet stores. If he wanted to add some color, you might buy him a roll of dog stickers, and he could add one or two to each flyer.

In very rare cases, the school might allow him to bring his dog into the school for a more realistic doggie demo. However, this would probably only be allowed in the very low grades and for a very short and monitored period of time. It is possible that the dog would have to be muzzled and the entire experience not exactly what your child had hoped for. Another possibility: give your child a video camera and let him make a video of himself giving the dog a bath, teaching it tricks, demonstrating dog care, etc. That way, he would achieve the same goal but with absolutely no danger or liability to the school or you.

CHAPTER FOUR

Whatever type of presentation or demonstration your child is asked (or volunteers) to do, just be sure he practices it at home a few times before he does it in front of the class. Practicing in front of a full-length mirror is another good technique. Teach him to continue despite mistakes and to not judge himself too harshly. One of the best ways to look at getting up in front of the class is that it is all practice for going out into the real world. Regardless of the grade he gets for a particular presentation, tell him that each time he gathers the courage to speak in front of a group, he will be that much more prepared for future academic and real-life speaking duties.

Sample Presentations

Third Grade Presentation

Grandma's Recipe for Roasted Pumpkin Seeds

Everyone knows that pumpkins are one of the best parts of Halloween. Kids love to carve funny faces in them, and adults like to use the yummy vegetable to make pumpkin pies. But let's not forget one of the tastiest and healthiest foods to come from pumpkins: their seeds! My grandmother taught me to dry pumpkin seeds and today, I'm going to share her recipe with you.

- First, scoop seeds from inside the pumpkin and spread them out to dry. Do not wash them. Pumpkin seeds can be dried at room temperature, in a dehydrator at 115 – 120 degrees Fahrenheit for 1-2 hours, or in a warm oven (200 – 250 degrees) for 3-4 hours. Stir them frequently to avoid scorching.
- When the seeds are dry, separate the fiber from the seeds. Try rubbing them between your hands. Place seeds in a colander and rinse them thoroughly with water. Dry seeds on absorbent paper.
- If you like salted pumpkin seeds, dissolve 1/4 cup salt in two quarts of water in a saucepan. Add the seeds and bring the water to a boil, then simmer on lower heat for about 2 hours. The seeds will turn gray. If you don't want salt, just leave it out, but cook the seeds as described.
- Drain the seeds and dry them well on absorbent paper.
- Use a bowl to mix 2 cups of seeds with one or two tablespoons of melted butter or oil. Sprinkle them with a teaspoon of regular salt, garlic salt, or onion salt, whichever you prefer. Or try other spices. (Writer's note: I tried this recipe with sesame seed salt and it was very tasty!)
- To roast the seeds, spread them in a shallow baking pan in a preheated 250-degree oven. Stir occasionally and roast until they are lightly browned and crisp. This usually takes 20-30 minutes.
- When the seeds are done, let them cool off, then seal them in an airtight container. They will keep for about 1-2 weeks that way. If you want them to last longer, you can freeze them.
- Oh, yeah – don't forget to eat the pumpkin seeds!!

PRESENTATIONS & DEMONSTRATIONS

Fifth Grade Demonstration Handout

Different Types of Gardens

A Winter Garden

Vegetables	Maturity	Growth	Companions
Artichoke	(120-150 Days)	M-48" diam.	
Beets	(55-100)	L-3"	Onions, broccoli
Broccoli	(90-120)	M-18"	Celery, dill, sage, thyme, mint, rosemary, lavender, beets, onions
Cabbage	(70-120)	L-24"	Dill, carrots, rosemary, beets
Carrots	(85 – 150)	L-2"	Peas, lettuce, chives, onions, rosemary, sage.
Cauliflower	(90-130)	L/M – 18"	Beets, onions, herbs
Celery	(160-200)	L/M-6"	Cauliflower, cabbage
Garlic	(110-140)	L-3"	Roses, raspberries (plant liberally throughout)
Lettuce (head)	(100-130)	L-12"	Strawberries, onions
Mustard	(50-70)	L-12"	
Onion, Bulb	(100)	L-3"	Beets, strawberry, lettuce
Onion, green	(100)	L-3"	Beets, summer savory, lettuce
Peas	(60-80)	M-3"	
Radish	(22-30)	L-1"	Peas, nasturtium, lettuce, Rhubarb
Spinach	(50)	L-3"	Strawberry
Turnips	(50-70)	L-3"	Peas

Garlic, Marigolds, Petunia, Tarragon: plant freely throughout garden.

Marjoram: plant here and there .

Yarrow: along borders, near paths, near aromatic herbs.

CHAPTER FOUR

Fifth Grade Demonstration Handout

Different Types of Gardens

A Spring Garden

Vegetables	Maturity	Growth	Companions
Beets	(60 Days)	L-3"	Onions, kohlrabi
Carrots	(65)	L-2"	Beans, peas, lettuce, leek, Rosemary, tomato, sage
Chard		M-12"	
Collards		M-14"	Sow indoors 4-6 weeks B4
Corn	(85-120)	H-12"	Cucumbers, pumpkin, squash
Endive	(90)	L-8"	Sow early, stands frost
Kohlrabi	(55-65)	L-4"	Beets
Leeks	(130 days)	L-4"	Onion, celery, carrot
Lettuce (leaf)		L-8"	Carrots, radishes
Mustard	(50-70)	L-14"	Sow early
Onion	(60)	L-3"	Scallion, beets, lettuce
Parsnip	(105)		Do not transplant
Peas	(60)		Carrots, Radishes Plant to trellis/vines
Pepper	(120-150)	M-18"	Sow indoors 4-6 weeks B4
Potato	(90-140)	L-12"	
Radish	(20-50)	L-1"	Lettuce, cucumber (Aids in repelling insects)
Spinach	(48)	LM-8"	Mint, nasturtium, parsley
Tomatoes		MH-18"	Chives, carrots Sow indoors 6-8 wks. B4
Turnips	(50)	L-3"	Peas

Herbs: Fennel, Sweet Marjoram, Fern Leaf Dill, Parsley
Flowers: Sweet Pea, Gloriosa Daisy, Gazania, Coreopsis, Forget-Me-Nots.

Spring Garden courtesy of UC Cooperative Extension.

Chapter Five

Research Papers

Learning to Read and Write

Forget the good old days when kindergarten was all about singing the ABC's, napping, snacking, playing, and learning to keep your hands to yourself. In the 21st Century, children entering kindergarten are expected to be fully prepared via preschool to listen and learn. And when I say "learn," I mean most school curriculums now include learning to read and write as part of the kindergarten requirements. Many schools are replacing the "look and memorize" approach to reading with the study of phonics. Children are taught the sound (or sounds) of a letter so that they can sound out an unfamiliar word. So instead of learning their "ABC's" as we did, they are more likely to point to the letters and say "Ah, ba, ca (hard c)." In fact, since I never learned the phonic symbols and sounds, I wasn't much help when it

CHAPTER FIVE

came to coaching my kids with their kindergarten and first grade reading assignments. I did my best to help them by reading to and with them as much as possible and by keeping lots of books in the house and making regular trips to the library. I'm fairly certain that at least a part of their reading education consisted of doing it "the old fashioned way," i.e., simply learning to recognize and memorize words.

As the students learn their letters and sounds in kindergarten, they are also guided to start reading and printing. You will be surprised by the types of academic tasks that four- and five-year-olds are expected to do. Not only are they given regular homework assignments, including projects, but during the first few months of kindergarten, they will be introduced to the concept of keeping journals. That's right! No time is wasted these days in preparing a child for their upcoming writing assignments. Little ones who can barely speak a sentence are required to write three sentences a day in a journal. One clever bunchkin in a class I taught recently filled an entire page with about ten phonetically-spelled words, then inserted three periods at various intervals to prove that she had indeed written three sentences. I gave her credit for being, if nothing else, a future poet.

If parents are paying any attention at all to their children's successive assignments as the elementary school years tick by, they will notice that the teachers are building an incremental foundation of writing skills which will enable the child to eventually meet the writing requirements of their upper level education.

In the primary grades, students are taught the actual mechanics of printing. By second or third grade, they are practicing cursive writing. Parents can always help by monitoring the inevitable writing practice, i.e., making sure that the loops are loopy and the tails properly descended on various letters. My daughter's first-grade teacher told me that, when your first-grader comes to you with a paper, regardless of the grade or legibility, a parent should always find something to compliment. In fact, she recommended that you point to a particular letter or number and say "I REALLY LIKE that 'S'! That's the best 'S' I've ever seen you make. You did a great job on that." She believed that meant more to a child than "Oh, that's a very good paper" or "Great job!" Try it! Your child will walk away with the biggest grin on her face.

RESEARCH PAPERS

As children begin to master the mechanics of writing, teachers begin encouraging children to write simple sentences. Gradually, they introduce the parts of speech, urging students to lengthen sentences by adding more descriptive and specific words. "I live with my mom and dad" becomes "I live in the blue house with my mom, dad, and a little black cat." Parts of speech are taught, retaught, and drilled repeatedly from second grade forward. What is a noun? "A person, place, or thing." What is a verb? "A word that describes an action."

Next comes the paragraph, which consists of three sentences, preferably all about the same topic. Paragraphs are followed by the three-paragraph composition, often explained to children as: "Tell me what you are going to say; tell me what you have to say; and tell me what you said."

The Purpose of Writing Exercises

Most children do not enjoy being taught the mechanics and structure of writing. In third grade, my son's teacher had a rule that vocabulary sentences had to be at least five words long. He made sure never to expend an extra ounce of energy by writing that sixth word. In fact, I often saw him counting his planned words on his fingers before writing and revising the sentence downward if it exceeded the minimum. And how we struggled with the idea of adding another sentence to a paragraph. His attitude was "Why ruin a completely good three-sentence paragraph if you don't have to?" While of course, Mom, the long-winded writer, always urged him to add just a few more details.

Trying to explain to a child why he has to keep writing sentences and paragraphs and compositions is a difficult, if not impossible, task for many parents. The truth is, many parents weren't required to do this much writing in the lower grades. I don't recall being asked to write any type of substantive paper until I was in ninth grade. The now popular "journal writing" was unheard of. Sometimes it seems as if my children are constantly writing some type of essay, composition, or report.

CHAPTER FIVE

Based on my interviews and surveys of teachers, the purpose of all these writing assignments seems to be very simple; by the time our children get to high school and college, educators hope that writing will be second nature to them. They won't have to suffer and struggle with *how* to write a paper. They will already know the basic structure and format expected by the institution. All of the journal writing, book reports, research papers, and impromptu essays will have paid off. In short, teachers hope that the continuous practice will result in the students at least feeling competent to tackle the larger projects that they will encounter in high school, college, and (yes) the workplace.

Research Papers, Levels of Report Writing

The first time your child is assigned a research paper, he or she may come home feeling very intimidated. Beginning in about the fourth grade, you can expect to see assignments that are variations of the type of research papers that a graduate student will turn in as a thesis. Fortunately, teachers are usually skilled in the art of introducing the different levels of report writing on a gradient that is painless and productive.

As I mentioned above, the first step to writing includes the multi-level process of learning to recognize, sound out, and write letters, then words, sentences, and paragraphs. Along with those skills, teachers reinforce related skills, such as reading, spelling, grammar, and syntax. Many of the elementary classrooms where I substitute teach seem to be focused on helping children develop and remember the same skills year after year. The standards set by districts and states focus on helping children not just to read, but to read with understanding. They want students to think about what they read. Writing assignments are intended to help the child coordinate their reading, writing, and thinking skills in a way that helps them relate to what they read. Finally, students are guided to develop writing skills that will allow them to easily compete in their upper level educational pursuits.

RESEARCH PAPERS

The goal of most educational institutions in the United States is to teach your child to write papers that conform with Modern Language Association (MLA) guidelines for writing research reports. For science reports, the report style follows the American Psychological Association (APA) style. The two styles are similar in many ways.

A complete research paper consists of several parts: a title page, an abstract (i.e., a short summary of what the paper is about); introduction; table of contents; methodology (i.e., how the student researched and prepared the information); the body; conclusion; and bibliography (see sample bibliography Appendix A, Norse Mythology Report). While that format may seem daunting to a college student, imagine how your fourth or fifth grader will feel when he or she first sees it? For that matter, imagine yourself as an adult faced with complying with this process if you've never before had to do it. My daughter had to write a formal MLA-style paper (excluding the methodology section) when she was in sixth grade. Her eighth grade science project research paper was written in full compliance to the APA style. Though she resisted and complained and procrastinated every step of the way, she ultimately produced two fine papers.

Parts of a Research Paper

Title Page

Abstract

Table of Contents

Introduction

Methodology

Body

Conclusion

Bibliography

CHAPTER FIVE

Elementary School Level Writing Assignments

Writing assignments in the primary grades (K-3) usually focus on the "body" section of a paper. In other words, younger students are generally not asked to produce the various other parts of the full research paper. They may be asked to prepare an outline before starting their papers, which include descriptive and informative paragraphs about one or more subjects. Their projects may include some written content, but it is usually only in the form of explanatory descriptions or photo captions. Book reports will be required to have a certain number of paragraphs, but teachers usually like to keep the overall length to an established maximum. When writing book reports, children are often given alternatives to the usual summarization of the story, e.g., they can draw a character, create a story board, act out a scene, or construct a pop-up book.

Since many elementary schools now end after fifth grade (at least in California), the emphasis in fifth grade is often focused on "getting the students ready for middle school." Teachers spend a great deal of time instilling in students the idea that they will be dealing with several teachers in middle school, each of whom is responsible for about 150 students. Fifth grade is their last chance to develop the proper study skills and to perfect their abilities to turn out the types of papers expected of middle school children. Required papers become a bit more complex. Teachers expect more pages, a deeper investigation of the topic, perhaps a bibliography. But these papers usually don't rise to the criteria of a full-blown research paper.

In fifth grade, besides the state report (described in Chapter Two and the Appendix), your child will probably be asked to prepare a few other research reports in different areas of study. For example, my daughter was assigned to do research papers on both vertebrate and invertebrate animals, complete with illustrations. In sixth grade, she did a full research report on Michelangelo. In both grades, she turned in long (10-15 pages!) typed papers with illustrations.

RESEARCH PAPERS

Choosing a Topic

Assisting your child in completing research reports in the lower grades usually involves teaching her to use the Internet and/or the library. Being old-fashioned myself, I find there is something comforting about taking my child to a traditional library and teaching him or her about encyclopedias, reference sections, and information desks. I like the feel of a heavy book in my hand, and I like flipping through the pages and running my finger down the entries to find what I'm looking for. It's like teaching a lost art to our technologically-evolved children. Most library card catalogues are now computerized, but you do find the occasional small-town library with an original hands-on card catalogue.

Regardless of the size of your town or city, I think libraries provide a learning environment that encourages the child to take him or herself seriously. In many of our local libraries, there are programs set up that enable older, retired people to tutor children for free. If you are not a whiz in a particular subject, perhaps you can inquire at the librarian's desk to see if anyone is available to help. In fact, most libraries have information or reference desks manned by people who are skilled in the art of finding exactly what you need. And believe me, there are probably very few topics that they haven't already helped someone research. Take advantage of your local librarians' knowledge and skills.

Of course, you can't write the child's paper for her, but during these first few efforts, it is very helpful for you to guide your student's research. For example, don't let your child pick a topic so large that he or she can't possibly cover it in five pages. Instead of "A History of the Civil War," suggest that your child research "The First Civil War Battle Fought in Virginia" or "A Famous Woman Who Helped the Union." The more specific the topic, the easier it can be to research. It's also possible to go too far in the other direction, i.e., choosing a topic so specific that you can't find anything at all about it. Recently, my son was assigned to do a Norse mythology report. He was given rather specific instructions (see Appendix, pp. 211-213), but his topic was literally drawn from a hat in class. Unfortunately, he drew the God

CHAPTER FIVE

"Vali," about whom very little was ever written. We went through book after book and website after website, usually finding the same paltry little paragraph or two about the Norse God of Love and Vengeance. How he ever managed to put three pages together on this guy, I'll never know. I think he'll do just fine in college. (We later found out that, had he asked, he could have changed his topic!)

If your child's topic yields no information after he or she has spent a decent amount of time searching, you may have to gently encourage a change of direction. Because a child may take this type of guidance as discouragement from a parent, I have sometimes written a note to the teacher, asking him or her to discuss the issue with my child. That takes a lot of stress off the parent-child relationship. Little Alison will come home with a *brand new* idea that she and the teacher concocted. You will still be welcomed as mentor and helper instead of viewed as the project discourager.

I love to browse through old issues of *National Geographic* for project ideas. It's a great place to find photos, and the articles are usually written in a very accessible style. Once your child finds an interesting topic, he can enhance his idea with research in encyclopedias, Internet websites, and books. Illustrative photos can be copied from the articles.

After your child makes a reasonable topic selection, you should encourage him to gather up eight or ten good sources of information, then spend an adequate amount of time reviewing the articles and data he has gathered. (Some teachers require a certain number of sources from each category, e.g., three websites, three books, three encyclopedias.) The art of note-taking should be thoroughly explained and demonstrated. Too often, children read the entire article and never write a thing down, not even a page number where they found something interesting. The child recalls that he read just what he need "somewhere, in one of those books," but can't recall which one. So a lot of time gets wasted as he shuffles through book after book trying to find the section or quote that he needs. Buy a package of those little colored Post-It Notes strips and show him how to use those to mark important or relevant parts of the books he is reading. Teach him to pick out the main ideas of paragraphs, pages, and chapters. Invest in making copies of short articles. Save helpful websites to your hard drive.

RESEARCH PAPERS

Organization

From kindergarten forward, organization is a big part of any project. Some people will tell you it is the heart of a successful effort. That is why teachers emphasize organization and usually do everything possible to help a child understand the need for it. There is nothing more frustrating for a teacher than to read a paper that contains a wealth of good information which has been poorly organized and, as a result, is unreadable. Very few of us can simply write a paper from start to finish and not have to go back and make adjustments, rearrange sentences, or change the focus of the report. Kids are loathe to do this. Organization can be as simple as arranging events in chronological order. A neatly-typed paper, with proper margins, page numbers, headings, and correct grammar and punctuation cries out to be read.

Help your child by teaching him to *first* clarify the assignment. Read the instructions yourself and waste no time getting answers to confusing or ambiguous directions. If your student is very young, he or she may have to be coached to work up the courage to ask the right questions. Sometimes it helps if you write, call, or visit the teacher. My kids have sometimes been terrified to ask a question because they somehow felt that asking a question about the assignment meant that either (a) the teacher will think he or she was stupid for asking, (b) the teacher will get mad at him for asking and take points off his final paper. You and I know these fears are mostly inappropriate and uncalled for, but, for the sake of your child's scholastic success, handle his fears gently and give as much help as possible up front. Remember, you will be the one who has to stay up late and help him fix the mistakes he could have avoided by asking questions.

Ideally, your child will have placed his photocopied research materials in labeled folders. Buy him one of those plastic pendaflex holders that are about eight inches deep by 12 inches wide and about a foot high, so that he can keep his various magazines, photos, and other research materials in one place.

CHAPTER FIVE

As the child reads through his various sources, he should make a preliminary outline of topics he wishes to cover in his paper. The standard outline procedure involves numbering the main ideas or sections with Roman Numerals (e.g., I, II, III). Within each section, subsections are headed with capital letters. Subsections within lettered sections are headed with numbers, followed by small letters, numbers in parentheses, etc. In the elementary and even in middle school, it is unlikely that a research outline would go beyond the first set of numbers.

Sample Outline

Kongo Kingdom

   I. Climate

      A. Coastal, Middle, and Plateau ecological zones

      B. Average temperatures in each zone

      C. Yearly precipitation in each zone

   II. Geography

      A. Boundaries

      B. Territories

      C. Middle Ecological Zone

      D. Mountain Ranges

      E. Coastal Areas

In the lower grades, it is more likely that the teacher will provide a general list of topics from which the child can choose. In fact, many teachers hand out very specific topics to individuals or groups and expect that the group will only research a topic from that list. (See Appendix for sample assignments.) Lists of acceptable science projects are also usually distributed by schools interested in avoiding chemical hazards, breakables, food allergies, live animals, dangerous electrical displays, etc. See Chapter Eight for ideas on how to come up with topics for papers and projects.

RESEARCH PAPERS

Staying on Schedule

A big part of organization involves staying on schedule. It is rare that a teacher will just hand out an assignment and say it is due in four weeks. A research paper has a twofold learning function. First, the child is given an opportunity to learn about the subject. Second, the child learns how to plan and execute the chosen project by performing all the relevant subtasks that are required for its completion. The first level relates to the grade in that subject that year. If properly taught and reinforced, the second set of skills stays with the child for a lifetime and will ensure his future success as a competent student, teacher, parent, and employee.

Timing is critical when it comes to gathering the source materials. Even if you have a huge library in your city, it is unwise to get overconfident and assume that everything you need will be there when you want it. We have gone looking for a book that is alleged by the computerized catalogue system to be on the shelves in the very library we are visiting, only to find that it has been lost, stolen, or wrongly shelved. Okay, so the next step is to try and order a copy from a cooperating library in the system. Uh-oh, there are seventeen copies available, but 12 of them are checked out, four are for reference purposes only, one is available, and you are fourth in line to reserve it. This could be a schedule-buster. Depending on your time-frame, you may have to visit a bookstore.

My son recently had an assignment to get the book *Seven Daughters and Seven Sons* by Barbara Cohen and Bahija Lovejoy. I knew for about a week that he needed it on the following Monday. On Saturday, we went to the public library and found that all available copies were gone. I spent most of Saturday and Sunday going from bookstore to bookstore, only to be told, "That must be a popular book. You're the fifth person who's been in here today asking for it." By Monday morning, I sheepishly had to drive for forty minutes to an inconveniently-located bookstore, then deliver it to my son's school just in time for the class in which he needed it.

CHAPTER FIVE

The moral of that story is that if certain materials are explicitly called for in a research assignment, grab junior and RUN, don't walk, to the nearest library or bookstore and order them, even if you have "lots of time" to do the project.

Another addendum to this thread of research report-writing: teach your child to TELL you when he or she gets an assignment. When they're young, well, even through fourth and fifth grades, you can pretty much go through their backpacks with impunity and find scrunched up assignments on the bottom. Once they enter middle school, such liberties are usually frowned upon. You have to rely on the child to keep you posted about their long and short-term assignments. If you have trained your child well (and the teachers do their part in this), he will be using his middle school agenda book to record his assignments on a daily basis. In some schools, the teachers give students the first few minutes of each class to write their assignments in their agenda books. Then they go around and award points to those who did it.

You can ask to see your child's agenda book every Friday and go over what he has written. If you note any references to projects, papers, or group meetings, ask to look at the assignment sheets, then proceed from there.

Like any major academic project or assignment, a research paper must be broken down into easily confronted parts and tackled on a piece-by-piece basis. Excluding science papers, the methodology section isn't always called for in elementary and middle school papers. In fact, the first time I had to write a methodology section was for my graduate thesis. And I must admit, it floored me for awhile. Aside from the methodology section, which determines how the topic discussed in the body of the paper was developed, researched, and written, most of the actual parts of the research paper flow from the body of the paper. For example, the abstract is a short summary (usually under 100 words) of the entire paper. Ideally, that section isn't written until the student has finished the paper. Likewise, the introduction is fully dependent on what follows. Those two sections, as well as the Table of Contents and Conclusion, cannot be adequately fleshed out until after the paper is finished.

RESEARCH PAPERS

The title page of the paper is generally limited to just that: the title centered about a third down the page and the child's name, class, class period, teacher's name, and date in the lower right corner. Sometimes, teachers accept pictures on the title page. Check first, but if this is the case, your child can either draw something, download a photo from the Internet, or you can invest in some of the pre-printed paper that can be found everywhere.

The abstract is usually the first page after the title page, followed by the table of contents. The table of contents follows a fairly standard format; some computer programs have a feature that automatically sets it up. Have your child do it last, so he puts the correct page numbers in.

The page length of the body of a paper depends entirely on what the teacher requested. She may say she wants a 10-page paper, but that 10 pages will include the body, plus all the other parts. If it isn't clear to your child how long the actual body of the paper needs to be, then he should ask and ask soon. Most teachers will deduct points if the paper isn't long enough, but some will deduct points if the paper is *too long*. The teacher only has so much time to devote to correcting papers. And she may not want to read 15 pages from any one child if she only asked for five (See Chapter Ten for more on following directions!)

I took a graduate level semantics course where the professor assigned us to write two 10-page papers. As I was finishing the first, it seemed like it might need a few extra pages. When I asked if he would accept more than ten pages, he said, "Sure, but no more than eleven." And by the way, ask the teacher where he wants the page numbers in the report (usually top right or bottom center).

CHAPTER FIVE

The introduction and methodology sections may or may not be included in middle school humanities assignments. If science fair projects call for research papers, they will most likely require those two parts, in particular the methodology, which explains why the student selected his topic and how he went about gathering data and performing his experiments to test his hypothesis.

The bibliography is a listing of source materials that is included at the end of the paper. If your student consulted twenty different sources, but only utilized thirteen of them to obtain research, then he should only list those thirteen. (See Norse Mythology Report pp. 211-213 for MLA bibliography formatting guidelines.)

Although many teachers still accept handwritten papers through middle school, I think it goes without saying that we are headed towards a time when teachers will expect all papers to be typed. I typed papers in college for money. But most kids these days are being introduced to the keyboard at a very early age. My children's teachers often indicated that it was okay for the parents to *type* the student's work, as long as the student actually did the work. In science projects, there is usually a section called "Who helped me and what they did," where the parents get credit for typing.

Some teachers prefer that papers be three-hole punched and placed in clear cover folders (the kind with built-in metal hasps). Other teachers make a point of telling children that they dislike notebooks because they don't stack easily. They prefer the simple "staple-the-corner" method. Train your child to always find out what the teacher expects before going forward with any plan.

Chapter Six

Schoolwide Projects

Volunteering in the Schools

For many parents, the phrase "school projects" includes much more than helping your child with his or her academic pursuits. Throughout the elementary and middle school years, and even into high school, you will be called upon to volunteer your time, expertise, and resources to assist your children's schools in promoting and presenting educational events, parties, fundraisers, sports events, field trips, talent shows, and even actually running the school via Parent-Teacher Associations (PTA) or Parent Teacher Organizations (PTO) and school committee membership. Because most schools today are underfunded and overpopulated, administrations struggle with the desire to provide the best for students while operating within a less-

CHAPTER SIX

than-adequate budget. From the first day of registration through graduation from elementary and middle schools, parents are needed, wanted, and actively recruited to provide backup personnel for everything from classroom assistance to school trip chaperones to processing paperwork and funds. Indeed, these "projects" may take up even more of your time than helping Eddie Junior build his medieval castle out of sugar cubes.

Volunteer Paperwork

Before you can begin to help out at your school in any way, you must complete certain paperwork which will be processed through your local school district. Depending on the district and sometimes the individual school, this paperwork may require fingerprinting, photos, TB Tests, and/or a background check. Most parents find this screening process to be annoying at best and downright intrusive at worst. Indeed, I have heard a lot of parents complain about the need for so much information just for the privilege of donating their time to their local schools.

It's true; no one likes to fill out paperwork, especially if they are only trying to do a good deed. But just think how badly you and everyone else would feel if the school or district adopted a more lax policy and allowed anyone and everyone onto the school grounds and into the classroom. Usually, schools try to make it easy on the parents by either doing a bulk mailing in the summer or sending the volunteer packets home with the kids on the first day of school. We all like to procrastinate, but my advice is to fill out and process the forms as quickly as possible. Many schools sponsor free TB tests during the first week or two of school, which can simplify your schedule.

Once you return the forms to the school, complete with your schedule of availability and preferred activities, the paperwork can still take up to a month to come back from the district. You will usually be issued some type of ID card to wear in the school when you are volunteering. This is not a perfect system, by any means, but it gives a measure of security to administrators and teachers who are ultimately responsible for your child's safety during school hours. It's much more pleasant for all concerned to have adults at your child's school identified by badges rather than to have to wonder constantly (or ask) about various unidentified adults walking around the school.

SCHOOLWIDE PROJECTS

Why Schools Need Parent Volunteers

To Promote School Spirit

"School Spirit" is one of those "I can't define what it is, but I know it when I see it" kind of feelings. If you've ever been in a school that had great school spirit, you know that it is a place where you feel welcome and where you get a sense of good will, productivity, and success just by walking inside. Students are interested and attentive, teachers and administrators are friendly, and the school is well-maintained and attractive. We'd all like our kids to wake up in the morning with an "I-can't-wait-to-get-to-school attitude." One way to encourage your kids to love school is to help your school build a strong and interactive support system. Schoolwide projects help promote school spirit by giving the children, their families, and school personnel a focus of shared goals and achievements.

One of the simplest ways that schools promote a feeling of community is by adopting a mascot. Our elementary school mascot was a whale, presumably because our school was next to the ocean. The whale appeared on school T-shirts, notebooks, pencils, pins, and other items which were normally offered for sale once or twice a year. Lovely whale murals were painted on walls throughout the school. Each year, the school yearbook boasted dozens of whale drawings created by students.

Another way that volunteer projects add to school spirit is that it gives parents a reason to *be at school* during school hours. Any of us who have dropped off a child at school on that all-important first day of kindergarten understand the feeling of dread that comes with leaving your baby in a roomful of strangers. Think how much more positive the experience is for your child if you wave goodbye and say, "Mom will be in the auditorium or cafeteria helping to organize the giftwrap sale or at a meeting for library volunteers." I remember the look of excitement on my son's or daughter's face whenever I happened to pass one of them in a school hallway or had to pop into their rooms to deliver fundraiser items. I personally just loved having children call out to me, "Hello, Mrs. Brett's Mom," as I carried out my volunteer duties.

CHAPTER SIX

I know it's a fact that not all parents are available to help during school hours. We live in a culture of single parents and two-income families, and everyone is busy. I was lucky. Running a business from home gave me the option of arranging my own schedule, so I was able to devote a lot more time to school activities than many other parents. But don't worry. There are many ways you can help, including on weekends and at home. Just keep reading.

To Promote a Sense of Citizenship

Many schools place a large emphasis on the development of children's sense of citizenship. In the classroom, citizenship is defined as "helping others," "being polite," "following the rules," and "respecting the rights and property of others." Monthly awards assemblies are held to honor students whose demonstrations of good citizenship merit recognition. Playground monitors often devise systems for rewarding students who pick up trash or are "caught being good" during recess. After a certain number of the reward slips are accumulated, the student is entitled to some type of prize, homework pass, or other privilege.

Schoolwide projects are an excellent venue for promoting a sense of citizenship among the students. Parents gain an opportunity to demonstrate the qualities of cooperation and productivity that teachers so highly value in the classroom. For example, many schools in our area have "school beautification days." Families show up on a Saturday morning to paint, pull weeds, organize library books, fix and patch things, plant flowers and trees, install computer equipment and wiring, etc. Children love these events. For one thing, they get to see the principal and teachers in jeans and sweatshirts. A camaraderie develops as people perform manual labor side-by-side, then sip lemonade and eat hotdogs on the patio. When the kids go to school the following Monday morning, they have a sense of belonging to a solid group made up of people working together (versus separate groups of students, teachers, administration). Such events allow everyone to feel they have a stake in the well-being of the institution.

SCHOOLWIDE PROJECTS

If you have a gift for landscaping, painting, carpentry repairs, or other outdoor types of work, you can donate your time at one or more of the school beautification events. Perhaps you have a large vehicle and can help move something to or from the school. I know, the district is supposed to be in charge of these things, but there's that old money thing again. That's why parents who can donate and plant a tree, trim hedges, sweep patios, paint the lunch tables, or move a file cabinet from one end of the school to the other are always welcome.

Community Outreach

Another type of school project that lends itself to a larger vision of the school's function involves community outreach. These projects can take the form of food, clothing, or gift drives during the holidays or ongoing projects, e.g., volunteering to tutor children in after-school literacy programs or offering free dance or pottery classes to students. Some schools set aside a portion of their annual fundraising efforts to grant charitable donations to families in need. Others take up collections in the event of tragedy among the school's or neighborhood's citizens.

As a parent, you might be called upon to lead or facilitate one of these annual drives or to offer your special talents in service to the children who might not otherwise have access to extracurricular activities. In the past, parents in our elementary school assisted after-school tutoring in the library, dance and voice lessons, coached cheerleading, and helped out in the computer and science labs, to name a few.

CHAPTER SIX

Community outreach is valuable because it sets an example for children – offering one's services for no reason other than the good of the community. In some schools, older students (fourth and fifth grade) are allowed to assist younger students with their homework during certain supervised times. They are also recruited to act as yard and hallway monitors, wearing special vests to indicate their placement. Of course, they are trained regarding their actual duties and taught not to overstep their authority. Either a teacher or parent volunteer meets with them on a monthly basis to discuss how to handle their "jobs." They learn to interact with younger children in the spirit of setting a good example and being helpful. This is just one example of how we can train children to participate in their educational systems. Anything we can do to promote a sense of community in our schools is worth doing.

Types of Schoolwide Projects

Joint Parent-Teacher Administration

PTA and PTO Boards

Every school has a parent-teacher organization of some type, usually called either a Parent Teacher Association (PTA) or a Parent Teacher Organization (PTO). Each year, parents elect a board of directors from among their dues-paying parent group. That board then works with the administration to oversee various school activities and fundraisers. Service on the PTA or PTO board of your school usually involves a major commitment of time and energy, as well as a gift for politics. Often, there is a small cadre of mothers (sometimes fathers) who work tirelessly to make sure things get done in a timely and organized fashion. If you have the time, I suggest you volunteer to be nominated or nominate yourself for one of the board positions. I've done it. It's an excellent way to keep track of *everything* that is going on in your child's school. It also helps you educate yourself (and others) regarding the dearth of funding for virtually everything related to schools today.

SCHOOLWIDE PROJECTS

PTA and PTO boards usually meet once a month to make decisions regarding school functions, bi-monthly membership meetings, fundraiser dates and products, volunteer recruitment, and endless other details of school management from the parents' point of view. Some schools have instituted a "parents' center" which seeks to assist parents with various economic, educational, or social issues or simply to provide a welcoming place for parents to congregate. Particularly in California, where a large number of families in any given school may speak a language other than English, the parents' center has proved invaluable in assisting parents who need extra guidance to understand the school paperwork, medical and educational requirements, and volunteer opportunities.

PTA and PTO groups also sponsor welcoming teas for parents and work with the administration to honor teachers during "Teacher's Week" and classified staff during "Classified Workers Week." In addition, they plan Back-to-School Night dinners and bake sales, oversee coupon drives, and sponsor enrichment assemblies for the students. Our PTO was instrumental in raising and designating funds and grant monies toward hiring a school librarian and science lab aide. Some of the money in our budget also went toward buying *Weekly Readers* for the kindergarten classes, sponsoring school beautification, and holding awards ceremonies for super volunteer parents.

When you decide to serve as a board member of the PTA or PTO of your child's school, you will be amazed to learn just how much money is raised each year via fundraisers and how that money is utilized to equip your school with computers, copy machines, and supplies, to pay aides' salaries, and to sponsor field trips, book fairs, and educational assemblies. You will also be astonished to learn how dependent the school administration is on your hard work and expertise.

CHAPTER SIX

School-Based Management Committees

Many schools also utilize the skills of parents by asking them to serve on local school leadership committees, which are charged with shaping school policy at the local level. Although such committee meetings can be boring (and seem to go on forever sometimes), they allow the parents to have input regarding the selection of textbooks, the formulation of the school's educational goals, and sometimes, even the hiring of teachers. If you have management or educational expertise or an interest in guiding your school's activities within district and state parameters, you can nominate yourself for one of the committees. The positions are elected, but there is rarely any competition. Once a month, you meet with the principal and other teachers and parents who have committed their time to resolving pending issues. There is usually some outside reading involved, but not a huge amount. For people who have business savvy but not much free time, committee service can be a very effective means of gaining a voice in your child's education.

PTA or PTO Board Positions

President

1st VP – Volunteer Coordinator

2nd VP – Enrichment

Treasurer

Secretary

Membership Chair

Parliamentarian

Hospitality Chair

School Historian

School Safety Chair

Library Chair

SCHOOLWIDE PROJECTS

School Spirit Fundraisers

Now let's talk about money. Schools need money and have had to find some very creative ways to raise it. Most of those ways involve selling something. Correction. They involve getting your children to sell something and getting you to handle the details. PTA and PTO boards are charged with deciding which fundraisers the school will participate in each year. Their decisions must necessarily be made far in advance, to ensure timely delivery of ordering materials, and, in some cases, to obtain sales perks from the company, e.g., a 50% profit on items sold if you commit to the fundraiser in June, versus a 45% profit if the board waits until September to make up its collective mind. This percentage difference may sound small, but 5% of a $20,000 fundraiser is $1,000.

Some fundraiser companies include prizes as incentives for good sales. Some make the school pay extra for those prizes (avoid these if you can; they are a royal ripoff). Some fundraiser reps come to the school for the kickoff assembly and really get the kids motivated to sell, sell, sell, and win, win, win the grand prize (often tickets to a favorite theme park or some type of electronic equipment). Other companies do little more than provide you with a flyer describing the product and order forms.

Although few school fundraisers are set in stone, it can be difficult to get the board to change from a company with which they have had lots of success to a different type of fundraiser. As a board member, you will find yourself and other board members wracking your brains for new and creative ways to make money for the school. Some of the various types of fundraiser projects that seem to come with the school territory are discussed below.

CHAPTER SIX

Sales of T-Shirts and Other School Logo Items

School spirit fundraisers require parent volunteers to organize paperwork, tally orders, collect and count money, and then reconcile orders, and deliver the items to students when they come in. One of the easiest school spirit fundraisers is the bi-annual T-shirt sale. The school usually makes a minimal profit on these items, but they do sell like wildfire. Parents and children alike will buy T-shirts, sweatshirts, windbreakers, golf-shirts, whatever, and proudly wear the school name and mascot. Other items, such as pencils, notebooks, pins, etc., usually go quickly as well. The school principal often buys up boxes of pencils, pins, folders, etc., and gives them as prizes and awards to children for excellence in academics and/or behavior.

This fundraiser generally involves a couple of weeks of work in the fall and another couple of weeks in the spring. You'll be very busy during that time, but it's a great way to get to know parents and teachers, compile a list of parents' phone numbers, and become an active member of your school community. You might even get a free T-shirt for your trouble.

SCHOOLWIDE PROJECTS

Big-Money School Fundraisers

Candy and Giftwrap Drives

One spring day when my son was in kindergarten and my daughter in second grade, I got a phone call from the volunteer coordinator (aka Board 1st VP) at our school. It seems I had put my name on a list of people who were volunteering to work on school fundraisers. Before that year, I had mostly volunteered in my daughter's classroom, leaving the fundraising headaches to others.

The volunteer coordinator assured me that she had more than enough people to work on the upcoming schoolwide candy drive. The only thing they needed was a volunteer to offer to chair the event. She explained that she herself had first chaired a candy drive only last year and went on to assure me how completely easy it was, even if I had never done it. Silly me, I was flattered. I said yes without a second thought. That was eight years ago. After that, I chaired every candy drive at that elementary school until my son graduated from fifth grade. That includes the extra, twice-annual (Christmas and Easter) fundraisers that were put on by the fourth and fifth grades to raise money for their fifth grade class camping trip to Catalina Island. I also assisted with the annual gift-wrap fundraisers held every fall, including teaching a few new "chair people" how to run a fundraiser.

Candy drives come in all shapes and sizes. Schools formerly seemed to favor the dollar-candy-bar drives, where a student signed out a $36 box of candy bars and was obligated to bring back $36. The school didn't care if Mom and Dad just wrote a check and ate all the candy bars in one sitting or if junior actually sold them one at a time. The point was, bring back the $36. If possible, sell multiple boxes. Many companies have since gone to the order form method of selling, even with one-dollar candy bars. Your child will take an order form around the family, the neighborhood, the church, or he will talk you into (yes, we've all done it) taking it to work. People will fill in their names, addresses, and phone numbers, plus the number of candy bars they want. Your child will collect the money up front and deliver his

CHAPTER SIX

order to the school. If the chairperson already has the candy on-site, you child will bring the candy home within a day or two. If not, on a designated end date, the chairperson will order the correct number of candy bars from the company. Then your child (read you) delivers the orders.

Other candy drives include those where four or five specialty items are offered during a particular season (e.g., chocolate Santas or tin soldiers or Easter eggs or rabbits) all for the same price. The ones I have learned to hate (and which seem to be becoming increasingly popular) are those where the student is given one (sometimes two!!) catalogues which are several pages long and which offer a multitude of items, with prices ranging from about $5 to $15. These are the candy drives that make parent volunteers quite grumpy. Giftwrap sales used to be sales where only giftwrap was sold. Now they have become giftwrap plus candles plus knick-knacks, plus candy, plus stuffed animals – you name it. The administration of these drives can get quite complicated because the companies often include one order form and catalogue for giftwrap and gifts and a second catalogue and order form for candy.

Normally, the promotional materials, order forms, envelopes, instructions, etc., for candy drives are provided by the candy company. The volunteer chair parent, in coordination with the PTO board and principal, has to decide when and for how long the drive will run, and when the candy will be delivered (usually a day or two before a holiday break). Next, he or she has to make phone calls to gather volunteers. Usually, a list is provided, which optimistic parents signed on the first or second day of school. By the time you call them, however, I guarantee that half of them have taken jobs, are about to have another baby, or thought they were signing up to allow their kid to *buy* candy. This is where you start calling all the people who chaired other events for which you volunteered. It's called politics.

At some point, you will have gathered enough volunteers to come in on a designated day (the day on which the candy sales envelopes are due). I recommend that you make the money due over a 2-3 day period. Even so, it continues to trickle in for a week, so give yourself plenty of lead time to get the order in and still keep your delivery date.

SCHOOLWIDE PROJECTS

If you are the chairperson of the drive, be sure you work out an explicit system for your volunteers regarding counting money and reconciling the orders. But be warned: no matter how organized you are or what system you come up with, the receipts will rarely balance. Think about it. You will be counting thousands of dollars in ones, fives, tens, twenties, and coins, *lots of coins*. I always included a note on the order form, asking the parent to tally the order and help the child count his collections, then write a personal check for the cash total. Some parents do that. Most don't. Be prepared to be frustrated. Count the money in a secure room. Never count money alone or let anyone else count money alone. Most school systems don't allow the receipts from a fundraiser to be taken off school grounds, so don't volunteer to count money thinking you can do it at your own kitchen table.

While it's nice to have a lot of help counting money and tallying order sheets, there is an old saying "Too many cooks in the kitchen spoil the broth." Better to have four or five people come in committed to stay until the work is done than to schedule people to pop in and out at half-hour or hour intervals. When you're done counting and have turned the funds over to the PTA treasurer or school secretary for deposit, you can forward your order to the fundraiser company sales representative, then sit tight and hope none of the checks the kids turned in bounce.

Fundraiser Guidelines

1. Volunteer to be chairperson.
2. Determine the kickoff date.
3. Contact the selected company for sales materials.
4. Make up sales packets for kids.
5. Send sales packets home with cover letter to parents explaining the entire procedure.
6. Call your volunteers and set a date to count money.
7. Collect orders from teachers on designated collection days.
8. Tally orders and reconcile funds.
9. Send order in.
10. Send reminder to parents about delivery date.
11. Contact volunteers for order distribution.
12. Distribute orders; award prizes; post top salespeople's names.

CHAPTER SIX

If a check bounces, the school secretary will inform you of the problem and you get to contact the parent. If it was a small check, simply withhold that part of the order until you get replacement cash. If the check was large enough to cover a child's entire order, hang onto the entire order until the parent brings the money in. Give a deadline for receipt of the cash. If the parent misses it, sell off the order to others at the school.

As the day of candy delivery nears, send home a reminder to parents whose children have large orders, so that they can be picked up. Many giftwrap and candy fundraiser companies deliver the orders already individually boxed. This makes your processing duties a lot easier, but you still have to have plenty of volunteers on hand to reconcile the orders, i.e., make sure that the order form matches the contents of each box. Depending on how much merchandise was ordered, this could be another full day's work. Make sure you have lots of moms on hand to help. Sign off each order sheet after checking the box. Kids sometimes have to ride the bus home and candy orders can shrink or disappear altogether. You have to have some type of verification that the child left with the order intact. (But you *will* inevitably end up replacing something for someone.)

Many candy and giftwrap sales net thousands of dollars for the school coffers. In a school of 500 children, you will usually see about 50% participation, but about 10% of the kids will sell 80% of the items. Our public elementary school of 500 children regularly sold $10,000 - $18,000 worth of candy or giftwrap per schoolwide sale. The school got 50% profit. When my daughter attended a private Christian school of roughly the same size, they held a giftwrap sale with the exact same company as my son's public school and grossed $42,000 in sales compared to our $18,000. That means the Christian school had $21,000 to invest in new playground equipment. The public elementary school spent its $9,000 profit on computers. Regardless of the difference in sales, the parents at both schools worked incredibly hard to make the drives successful.

SCHOOLWIDE PROJECTS

Walkathons

During the past 5-10 years, walkathons have become a popular way for kids to raise money for either their schools or some designated charity. These events can qualify under the heading of either school spirit, good citizenship, and/or community outreach. Because of transportation problems in larger cities, they are usually held during school hours (e.g., during physical education periods), though some smaller towns still schedule them for Saturday mornings. The idea of a walkathon is that the child collects pledges from friends, neighbors, strangers, whoever. These people agree to pay X amount for every lap the child does.

Getting the child's sheet filled clearly calls for parental assistance. Your youngster can't go door-to-door collecting signatures alone. Primary grade students may not even fully grasp the concept of the walkathon fundraiser. Once the pledges have been made and the child completes his or her event, there is the all-important step of actually collecting the money for the verified laps.

Parents, be warned; it is wise to check on the size of the track that the child will actually be asked to walk. A friendly but unsuspecting neighbor may agree to pay $1 a lap, only to learn that the child completed 50 laps of a rather small track. Most of your neighbors, no matter how good-intentioned, will balk at making such a large donation.

Some schools vary the walkathon by sponsoring "jump-a-thons" where the child is verified has having jumped, hopped, or skipped for certain numbers of times. You would be amazed at the level of endurance of some elementary school children. Be a responsible parent – find out what your kid is really signing your neighbors up for *before* it comes time for them to pay up.

CHAPTER SIX

On the other side of the walkathon coin, there is usually a tremendous need for parent volunteers to monitor the event, count laps, tally sheets, collect and count money, etc. You might even be asked to recruit other volunteers. It's usually not more than a day or two's worth of commitment, and it's fun to get out there with the kids when they are committed to raising money for their school or a needy organization.

Rummage Sales

It may sound far-fetched, but one good schoolwide rummage sale can bring in thousands of dollars. My daughter attended first grade in a Colorado Springs school, where the annual rummage sale was a huge event. Flyers went out during the first week or two of school, asking for donations to be made during a particular two-week period. The sale was held in October. As the donations came in, droves of parent volunteers spent many hours tagging items. A large bake sale was also held in conjunction with the two-day (Friday and Saturday) rummage sale.

By the day of the event, the school yard, the auditorium, and the cafeteria were literally full to the brim with secondhand items, including clothing, toys, appliances, furniture, you name it. To avoid confusion, several "cashiers" worked in one room. Lots of dads were on hand to carry furniture and large items to customers' cars. When all was said and done, the sale netted over $4,000 for the school, all profit. This type of sale can be promoted as a "fall beautify-your-home and help-your-school" event. Some parents who might not be interested in other types of volunteering will be thrilled to participate in a rummage sale. Just think, you'll get first dibs on buying stuff!

SCHOOLWIDE PROJECTS

Holiday Parties

Halloween, Thanksgiving, Christmas, Easter, Etc.

Photos by Kathie Weir

Halloween Party

Although Halloween has fallen into disfavor in many parts of the country, a great number of schools still celebrate this holiday in one way or another. The traditional Halloween festival with games, costumes, and parades is a favorite among elementary school children. By the end of September, some brave set of parents has volunteered to organize a half or full day set of events that result in every child's winning a lot of candy and silly plastic items. In recent years, schools that do celebrate Halloween seem to be following a trend to make October 31st a half school day, which is a good idea as far as I'm concerned. Many schools also have arranged to make November 1st one of those euphemistically named "non-pupil" days. In other words, the teachers have to go to school, but the children don't.

Generally, the PTO board has provided some funding, though parents may also be asked to contribute some nominal amount to cover costs. Traditional Halloween celebrations may also involve requests for donations of baked or store-bought goods. Children are frequently allowed to come to school in costume, to have parties in the classroom, to take their turns in the auditorium, where games such as throwing beanbags, cakewalks, spinning wheels, etc. are set up. Parents who enjoy getting dressed up in costumes usually run these games. If you are oriented towards the theatrical, this is your chance to have some fun with the students and probably please your own children. Afterwards, parents get to clean up the mess!

CHAPTER SIX

Photos by Kathie Weir

Halloween Party

Photos by Kathie Weir

Last Minute Santa Claus Costume, modeled by Ben Manzella

Thanksgiving and Christmas seem to get rolled into one big blur of holiday art projects, classroom parties, and theatrical productions by various classes. You may get tagged for any or all of the duties. When my son was in third grade, his teacher came up to me about three days before their Christmas production. "I just want to thank you for offering to let us use your Santa Claus suit," she said.

"Santa Claus suit? Did I miss something?" I replied.

"Yes, Brett said you could let us borrow the one you have at home."

The only problem, I told his teacher, was that I didn't have a Santa suit at home and had no idea what made my third grader think I had. Well, actually, I did know what made him think I had a suit. Based on the previous three years, he just assumed I could come up with anything he needed anytime he needed it. He simply forgot to mention what he needed.

SCHOOLWIDE PROJECTS

The teacher looked so disappointed that I immediately ran out and bought red and white felt, then rushed home to stitch one up. I found red pants in a K-Mart on sale for $3 and had black boots, a belt, and a Santa hat at home. I even found a Santa beard at a local costume store. The play went off without a hitch, and my son thought I was a heroine.

Valentine's Day, St. Patrick's Day, and Easter follow pretty much this same routine. Teachers want to give the kids a fun time, but they are swamped with all their teaching and administrative duties. They need your help. Plan ahead, so that you can simply present your idea to the teacher a couple of weeks in advance.

Harvest Festival

A few years ago, I had this bright idea to substitute an "educational" event for the Halloween festival at our school. Having had a farm background myself, I thought it would be worthwhile to prepare a huge interactive demonstration/workshop setting where children could learn about the concept of harvest. Somehow, I garnered enough support within the PTO board to do away with that year's Halloween festival and substitute my plan.

The basic idea was to demonstrate to children how food got from the ground to their plates and what types of events occurred during traditional

Photo by Carole McLean

Harvest Festival Displays

harvest times. I called in every favor from every parent possible to organize my event. We had one woman who sponsored a "Bees-to-Honey" display; another handled the "Pumpkin-to-Pie" and "Apple-to-Pie" tables, complete with tastings. Children learned to make butter by shaking cream in little babyfood jars.

CHAPTER SIX

Photo by Kathie Weir

Photo by Carole McLean

Harvest Festival Activities

One mother used her expertise to organize a "corn-husk doll-making" workshop, which surprisingly went over as well with the boys as it did with the girls. The children colored farm scenes and observed antique kitchen equipment. Another mom with quilting expertise gave quilting demonstrations. Many parents showed up dressed in period clothing.

Photo by Carole McLean

African Drummer, Darrell Cox; Mary Piepenbrink, Harvest Festival Quilter

The school also sponsored two assemblies in conjunction with the three-day Harvest Festival: one was by a storyteller and African instrument maker who enchanted the children with his harvest stories. The other was an American folksinger. By the end of those three days, parent volunteers were worn out, but very proud. We had pulled together an amazing learning environment for our school, with a very small budget and lots of parent power and creativity.

SCHOOLWIDE PROJECTS

Country Faire

Photo by Kathie Weir

Traditional Country Faire Costume modeled by Sierra Weir (purchased at Salvation Army for $3.00)

My daughter spent her first two years of middle school in a K-8th Grade Lutheran School which was modeled more on the traditional elementary school. Having religious objections to Halloween, they sponsored a yearly "Country Faire" which offered the kids a chance to dress up in certain specified costumes (e.g., as cowboys, farmhands, country ladies, farm animals, vegetables, etc.). Of course, none of the usual Halloween ghosts, witches, vampires, or devils were allowed, but the kids at least got to express themselves.

The children spent the entire day outside, participating in everything from pie-eating contests (I was *not* happy to learn that my daughter wolfed down an entire pie) to rope climbing, pumpkin decorating, and three-legged races. This is another style of celebrating the fall season that seems to work well for both parents and children alike. Just remember, such events don't work *at all* without the time and energy of parents dedicated to enhancing their children's education with hands-on experiences.

CHAPTER SIX

Greek Day, Roman Day

In sixth grade, it seems like kids have a lot of leeway to develop their sense of drama as they study the great civilizations of history. Since the Ancient Greek, Roman, Egyptian, and Chinese civilizations were so richly textured in terms of color, design, cultural pageantry, and ritual, it is no wonder that teachers seize on these eras as an opportunity to not only teach the children about these ancient cultures, but to actually live them.

Photo by Sierra Weir

Dodson Gifted and High Ability Magnet Middle School Teachers, Karen Kromer and Anthony Louros join in the Spirit of Greek Day

Moms, get ready; this is where the costumes come in. Remember toga parties in college? Well, now, at least one or two days a year in sixth grade are devoted to wearing togas and participating in games that were traditionally played in Greek or Roman times, producing artwork, and eating traditional foods. In some schools, the dress-ups involve Egyptian or Chinese cultures. Usually, the teacher (or more often, teachers) prepare an entire unit on the relevant historical period that covers English and social studies, and sometimes includes math and science as well. Students may be assigned both individual and group projects. In my son's case, he had to make a Greek vase and write up a report on some aspect of Greek culture. He also had to work with a group that developed a "Greek TV" news report. On "Greek Days" at the school, everyone, including the teachers, dressed up in togas and participated in events designed to enhance their understanding of life in ancient Greece.

Photo by Anthony Louros

My Son, the Greek

SCHOOLWIDE PROJECTS

Book Fairs

Book Fairs are usually sponsored by the PTA or PTO twice a year. Many are sponsored by Scholastic, which provides books and everything else needed – except the labor. Portable book displays are set up either in the library or auditorium for a one-week period. Children are allowed to visit the book fair during designated class periods, as well as during their lunch, recess, and after-school times. Children are able to purchase award-winning books, educational computer games, and book-related items, such as bookmarks, posters, and games, at excellent prices. Parents can send their children in with a few dollars to spend or sign a check with a "Not to Exceed" amount in the corner. Students enjoy the opportunity to make independent shopping choices.

Without parents, many Book Fairs simply wouldn't happen. For one solid week, two or three parents must be available to run the book fair from early in the morning until school closes. In our school, they also kept the bookstore open for one evening until 7:00 p.m., to allow the parents an opportunity to do their own shopping. If you are unable to volunteer on a continuous basis, you can pick one week each semester to coincide with the book fair and contribute many hours in one block. It's fun to spend the time with other parents. You get an opportunity to do your Christmas or other gift shopping in a pleasant environment, and you also have time to meet your children's teachers, friends and classmates, as well as some of their parents. Book fair profits are usually used to enhance the library or other book-related school needs.

Photo by Kathie Weir

Scholastic Book Parade Fair

Often, during book fair week, the school will find authors to come in and talk to kids. Or they will sponsor a "dress as a character" parade, where kids get to come to school dressed as one of their favorite characters, march around, and go to the microphone to talk about the book and character. One year, my daughter's favorite book was *The Paperbag Princess*. That was a fairly easy costume to come up with.

CHAPTER SIX

Classroom Assistance

Classroom Helper

Photo by Sierra Weir

Art to Grow On Calendar Depicting One Classroom's Artwork for Each Month

Imagine being a teacher running a class of 20-35 students all by yourself? In the lower grades especially, parents are generally welcomed as volunteers, particularly around holidays when there are extra classroom projects, parties, plays, and singing performances. Many teachers arrange to have one or two parent helpers in the room every day. My daughter's first grade teacher had moms coming in on one-hour shifts every day after lunch. She would send four or five kids to a table in the back and the moms would help them cut things out, finish an assignment, or drill math concepts. If there are enough moms in the room, the teacher might even ask for each mom to work individually with a student for 15 minutes at a time.

If you have special talents, your child's teacher may allow you to take over a lesson or two (under the teacher's supervision, of course). I know one mom who is a potter. Each year, her son's class was treated to a special unit on making pottery, complete with a hands-on project. Some parents who have exceptional computer skills like to volunteer during their children's computer lab. There is definitely something for everyone in the school projects department.

SCHOOLWIDE PROJECTS

In our district, a local artist started a program called "Art-to-Grow-On" in the elementary schools. It was developed as an offshoot of "Art at Your Fingertips," an organization which has put together an instructional video regarding how to start a similar program in your school. Contact *artcenter @palosverdes.com* for more information. Each year, parents who volunteer to be "docents" in the program are trained to deliver and supervise four art projects which are designed to enhance the child's knowledge of art history and technique. Even though every student in every class does the same project, the results are astonishingly different and original. Art to Grow On volunteers have also developed a yearly fundraising event; they sell calendars featuring collages of the artwork of each grade. The money is put back into the program for the purchase of more and better materials.

Workroom Assistant

If you aren't suited by temperament or schedule to classroom duties, you can assist in the teacher's workroom by laminating projects or teaching materials, cutting things out, and preparing kits for classroom projects. Often, a teacher has little cutting, stapling, or organizing projects that you can work on at home. All you have to do is ask. Some teachers need help correcting tests or assembling portfolios for the kids to display on Back-to-School Night. Anything you do will be sincerely appreciated by our incredibly dedicated and sadly overworked teachers.

CHAPTER SIX

Career Day

Most elementary and middle schools have at least one Career Day or Career Week per semester. The administration seeks out parents who have a variety of jobs and careers to make rotating presentations to children who have expressed an interest in their respective fields. You can either help organize the event, by recruiting people to make presentations, setting up the career stations, scheduling the class or group rotations, or providing refreshments. Students are usually allowed to select three careers from a list of available speakers. Then, on the prescribed day, they visit that person's table or work station for a fifteen- or twenty-minute presentation about that specific career choice. Children can ask questions, e.g., "How long would I have to go to school to be an engineer?" or "What is the difference between a teacher and a professor?" or "Is it difficult to be a mechanic?"

Again, this is a very once-in-awhile event, but one that you might be able to contribute to if you can't make a weekly or more regular commitment of time. About 50% of the families in my kids' elementary school were from a nearby military base, so we always had lots of captains, sergeants, FBI agents, scientists, and pilots participating in our Career Day. Since we live on the coast, we also had our share of fishermen, longshoremen, artists, and boating experts. I represented writers at career day. Such contributions may not seem like much in terms of time, but every new career option that a child learns about opens one more door of possibility for his or her future. I think Career Day volunteers are performing a very worthwhile service to our kids.

SCHOOLWIDE PROJECTS

Yearbook Staff Advisor

This is another one of those "didn't we only do this in high school?" kind of activities. Yes, we did only have yearbooks in high school, but now the process starts in kindergarten. And since kids in the lower grades can't really participate at the level of teenagers, there is a need for a mom or two or three to run this show. Generally, the school selects a professional photography studio and/or printer to actually produce the finished product. But the yearbook advisor is responsible for all the little extras, including photos of special events, impromptu photos, cover art, advertising sales, organizing yearbook orders, and distribution.

Photo by Sierra Weir

Elementary School Yearbooks

CHAPTER SIX

The advisor often conducts a drawing contest in the school and selects the cover art from among the winners. Students will be handed a form with specific instructions of what to draw, e.g., a whale. Then an independent judge selects the winning entry. The yearbook advisor usually finds a place for all of the entries throughout the pages of the yearbook.

Yearbook sales are conducted in a manner similar to other fundraisers. Of course, the profit margin is slim, because it is more of a school spirit event than anything else. Most elementary school yearbooks are softcovered and sell for under $10. Middle school yearbooks (usually supervised by a faculty advisor and prepared by students) can sell for up to $30. On the day the yearbooks come in, kids are scurrying all over the playground, getting their friends and teachers to sign their yearbooks, just like in high school.

I'm sure I haven't included all of the different ways that schools will utilize parent volunteers. There are so many areas where our help is needed and wanted. While the academic component of your child's school experience is critical, we can't ignore the many aspects in which our time, expertise, and labor are needed and wanted to support the greater educational goals of our schools and communities. From digging in the dirt to teaching arts and crafts to baking and serving treats to serving on committees, every parent can find a niche for service to our local schools.

Chapter Seven

Parties, Picnics, and Off-Campus Trips

School Parties

I don't know about you, but I actually don't recall having very many classroom parties when I was a child. These days, though, classroom parties are as much a part of the curriculum as reading, writing, and arithmetic. Early in the school year (either on the first day or during back-to-school night), teachers will have sign-up sheets out for parents to volunteer for different activities. One or two parents (usually moms, but sometimes a dad) will take on the duties of "Homeroom Parent." Thereafter, he or she will be responsible to arrange the various classroom parties throughout the year. That includes calling other parents to assign duties, coordinating times and menus with the teacher, helping the teacher supervise the party, and cleaning up afterwards.

CHAPTER SEVEN

Party schedules may vary from school to school and even from one classroom to the next. Most public elementary schools celebrate the following holidays with some type of schoolwide or classroom participation: Halloween, Thanksgiving, Christmas, Valentine's Day, Easter, Memorial Day, and End-of-School or Culmination (from fifth grade). The party celebrations seem to taper off in public middle schools. However, my daughter attended a private middle school for sixth and seventh grade and they seemed to be having parties every other week.

Many of the school fundraisers also involve giving parties as a reward for high sales performance by either individuals or classrooms. If a student is the top sales person, part of the prize may be a party for his or her classroom. Likewise, some schools and teachers reward classroom achievement with parties: ice cream parties, pizza parties, root-beer float parties; you name it. The level of parent participation may vary, but once you are on the teacher's list of classroom helpers, be prepared to answer the numerous calls you will get.

Over the course of a year, a parent may also be asked to contribute party food or favors for Back-to-School and Open House nights, Teacher Appreciation Week, science fairs, and any number of school events. In middle school, my daughter actually got extra points for her science project for the food we donated. I think the maximum number of extra points was 200 for two six-packs of soft drinks and a large bag of potato chips. (No comment.)

It may sound odd in some parts of the country, but in California, there has been a trend away from bringing home-baked goodies to school, due to largely unsubstantiated fears about spreading disease. In a way, that makes it easier on parents who may not have the time or the inclination to do a lot of baking. Some parents still want to bring their home-baked specialties to school. To my knowledge, this practice hasn't been banned. So if you like to cook, don't stop. I don't know of any kid who will walk away from home-baked cookies, fudge, or cupcakes. Just remember, peanuts, peanut-butter, and peanut oil are now on the "forbidden" list in most schools, due to potentially severe reactions of those who may be allergic to peanuts.

PARTIES, PICNICS, & OFF-CAMPUS TRIPS

If you sign up to help with parties by providing food, drinks, and paper products, it is always wise to keep a stash of those items on hand. Christmas may seem like a long way off in September, but those holidays have a way of sneaking up on us. After the first year or two of pre-school and kinder-garten parties, I wised up and began stockpiling paper plates and cups, napkins, plastic utensils, and even gallon jugs of apple juice and punch. If you keep your eyes open for buy-one-get-one-free sales and make good use of coupons, you can pick up many of these items for practically nothing, then become known around school as the person to count on in a pinch. Of course, it's not practical to buy cookies or cupcakes too far in advance, but individual bags of popcorn, chips, and pretzels can be stored for awhile. Boxed juices and single-serving puddings, fruit-cups, and applesauce that don't require refrigeration are great to keep on hand.

Stock Up on Party Supplies

1. **Paper plates**
2. **Paper cups**
3. **Napkins**
4. **Plastic utensils**
5. **Brown lunch bags**
6. **Sealable sandwich bags**
7. **After-holiday sale decorations**
8. **Gallon bottles of fruit punch or juice**
9. **Paper table cloths**
10. **Party hats or favors as appropriate**
11. **Single serving snacks**
12. **Balloons**

Don't get carried away and try to freeze holiday-themed candy for a year. That definitely won't work. But holiday favors, e.g., little Santa Claus figures, ghost erasers, Valentine's doilies and hearts, or plastic Easter eggs can be purchased at after-holiday sales for next year's parties.

CHAPTER SEVEN

As long as you don't mind being in a room full of excited kids, monitoring classroom parties is a fairly low-stress way to fulfill your parent volunteering duties. Sometimes, besides party food and paper products, the teacher might ask a parent volunteer to come up with a little party activity for the kids to do. I usually opt for some type of holiday-related crafts project. For example, at Halloween, you can buy some of those miniature pumpkins and then let them either paint or decorate them. You can provide little bits of yarn or pipe cleaners for hair, sticky felt from which to fashion eyes, nose, and mouth, glitter glue for decorative purposes, construction paper to make hats, etc. You can even buy little hats at crafts stores and use fabric scraps to make ties or bows to pin on the pumpkin.

Photo by Kathie Weir

Decorated pumpkin

As the party winds down, be sure to leave the last five or ten minutes for the kids to clean up the room. Give the kids each a brown paper lunch bag or sealable plastic bag in which to take home their loot from the party. Make sure all the desks are wiped clean and floors are spotless. Otherwise, the school maintenance people tend to get cranky about classroom parties. Bring home all your extra supplies and put them away for the next party.

Picnics

Picnics are a lot like school parties, except they are generally few and far between. If you live in the milder climates, you may have to cater more picnics each year. Generally, picnics are held in the early fall or during the spring, towards the end of school. Whether it is an annual schoolwide picnic, held on a weekend, a picnic held for fifth graders to celebrate the end of their elementary school years, or a simple classroom outing to a nearby park, the key to picnics is to keep it simple.

PARTIES, PICNICS, & OFF-CAMPUS TRIPS

Photo by Kathie Weir

School picnic fun

Instead of getting everyone to bring food, have each student bring in three or five dollars and buy a few simple menu items at the grocery store. For our fifth grade picnics, it was always the same: hot dogs, hamburgers, beans, potato salad, chips, sodas, and watermelon. Nothing exciting, but it doesn't have to be. Kids are naturally thrilled by the thought of getting out of a day of school, and we all know that food tastes much better outside. Teachers usually supervise the games. Parents are mainly responsible to make sure the food arrives, cook and serve it, and clean up afterwards. Also, we help maintain order and count heads when it's time to leave. Picnics are often arranged so that the kids can walk to the park, but transportation of sports equipment, portable barbecues, blankets, etc. may be required. And don't forget the First Aid kit; someone always needs it.

Educational Excursions

Another aspect of volunteerism that some parents prefer involves chaperoning the children on a variety of educational excursions that can last anywhere from a few hours to a few days. To do this, you will, of course, have all your paperwork in order, as required by your local district. You will also have to be patient, resilient, adventurous, vigilant, and have a very good back for those bumpy school bus rides. (Who designed those seats, anyway?)

When I was in school, we thought we had been handed the world if the school provided bus transportation to away football and basketball games. Today, it seems like some schools deliver half of the students' education offsite. Well, not really, but, depending on the school your child is in, the travels can get hectic.

CHAPTER SEVEN

Field Trips

Field trips are a part of almost all school curriculums. If you are an over-protective parent like I am, you probably will feel safer accompanying your primary-grade children on field trips. I couldn't bear the thought of my five-year-old wandering away from the group in the Museum of Natural History. It's not that I didn't trust the two teachers who were involved or the other parents who had volunteered. In fact, most of them were going for the same reason I was: safety concerns. It's just that I have an over-active imagination which could only be quieted if I was actually present during the trip. Besides, I've gotten lost in museums a few times myself.

Photo by Sierra Weir

Autry Museum of Western Heritage

Usually, field trips are organized well in advance and trip slips are sent home for signatures. If it is a local trip for a small class (for example, a swimming party at the local military base), the teacher will often organize carpools. This is where owning a van comes in handy. The trip slip will detail the time frame, location, mode of transportation, and whether or not your little one will need a bag lunch or money to buy lunch. In addition to a trip slip, if parents are providing transportation, they have to produce insurance information and copies of their drivers' licenses way in advance. This may seem like an annoying detail, especially if the five kids who go in your car are the same ones who carpool with you every day. However, the school is responsible for each child's safety during school hours. If a school allows a parent to transport children in a private vehicle on a school-sponsored trip, the school must validate that parent's credentials in order to protect the school, the parent, and the child.

PARTIES, PICNICS, & OFF-CAMPUS TRIPS

LOS ANGELES UNIFIED SCHOOL DISTRICT
**PARENT'S OR GUARDIAN'S PERMISSION FOR A FIELD TRIP
AND AUTHORIZATION FOR MEDICAL CARE**

You will fill out lots of trip slips

Some schools arrange for the cafeteria to provide bag lunches for children who usually buy their lunch at school. If your child usually brings his or her lunch, the school will request that you send a bag lunch w/ only disposable items, i.e., no lunch box, thermos, or other items that have to be returned. It's just too easy to lose such items.

As a chaperone, you will probably be assigned to supervise a group of children (usually 4-5 little ones or as many as 10-12 older students) as you tour the museum or factory or fire station or while you eat your lunch at a nearby park. Your child will most likely be assigned to your group. For your own sanity, and to avoid having to yell, "Hey, you in the green shirt," I suggest you bring along a box of name tags and a marker pen. If the teacher didn't think of them, he or she will love you for it. In fact, all of the parents will think you are pretty smart for remembering such a common-sense safety item. The school office might even have name tags with the school name and number already printed on them. A cell phone is also a handy tool on field trips.

Super Parent Field Trip List

1. **Lunches for you and your kid**
2. **Moist towellettes (for sticky fingered-kids)**
3. **Name tags and marker**
4. **Cell phone**
5. **Magazine**
6. **A small daypack to carry things in**
7. **List of phone numbers, including the school and teacher's cell phone numbers**
8. **Sweater or jacket**
9. **Camera**
10. **Tissues and extra napkins**
11. **Pencil and paper**
12. **Ear plugs**

CHAPTER SEVEN

Regardless of the age of the children who are attending the field trip, prepare to be frazzled by the end of the day. The bus ride itself will make you wonder why you ever agreed to go. The bus is usually too hot or too cold. The kids are noisy (although many schools now allow kids to bring tape or CD players to occupy themselves). Unless you live in a very wealthy district, you will be riding on buses with non-adjustable seats, so bring something soft to lean your head back. Most school district bus drivers run a pretty tight ship, but the noise level is still fairly high. Ear plugs help (I'm serious – just remember to take them out when you get off the bus). Take deep breaths and try to keep the kids in your immediate area under control with stern looks and gentle admonitions. Leave the yelling to the teachers and bus drivers.

Be prepared to schlep four or five little ones in and out of restrooms. If the children are really young, bring envelopes and take charge of their money. I don't know why, but schools often indicate in their permission letters that children should bring money for gift shop items. There is nothing quite as chaotic as a couple of classrooms of first or second graders turned loose in a museum gift shop. In fact, many gift shops have tight controls on gift shop entry: every four children must be accompanied by a responsible adult. Helping the kids decide what to buy is always an experience in creative management. And at least one child will end up in tears because he or she either forgot to bring money, doesn't have enough to buy what he wants, or can't make up his mind before you have to drag him out of the gift shop and jog to the bus.

One problem that some museums face, particularly in large cities, is that there are often too many class trips to accommodate. Rather than turn anyone away, they severely limit the length of the tours. Your group may be allowed as little as one hour to tour a huge museum. The result is often cranky kids who want to linger over certain exhibits while you and the docents rush them through. It is wise to explain to the children beforehand that they will only see a small part of the museum this trip, but that they can have their parents bring them back to take a more leisurely tour later.

PARTIES, PICNICS, & OFF-CAMPUS TRIPS

Butterfly Sanctuary at Museum of Natural History

Photo by Sierra Weir

If you have any input into the field trip decisions, you might suggest some of the smaller, less well-known, but often good quality museums for field trips. We live on the California coast, where there are dozens of small maritime and marine museums, whale-watching tours, garden or beach walking tours, and other less time-intensive, but every-bit-as-exciting destinations. Many of these smaller facilities are free or virtually free, which can be a big help for schools on tight budgets. Spend your summer doing a little research on local attractions, then present a list of suggested destinations, complete with times, prices, and distances. The principal and teachers are always looking for new ideas; you will immediately be placed on their "Volunteer Star" list.

Field trip to Universal City

Photo by unknown

Did I mention that many schools now take children on year-end trips to places like Disneyland, Magic Mountain, water parks, and the like? Sometimes, those trips are offered as prizes to kids who did well academically or raised over "X" amount selling candy or other fundraising items. The fun trips are often organized on weekends, and they are the ones that I always tried either to talk my children out of or got their father to take them. I simply don't do rollercoasters and waterslides. And the thought of losing someone else's kid in an amusement park is just not my idea of fun. On the bright side, I will say that I have let my daughter attend a couple of theme park events, and she came back no worse for the wear. I just tried to keep busy on those days.

Field trip to the beach

Photo by Kathie Weir

CHAPTER SEVEN

School-Sponsored Camps

School-sponsored camping trips were unheard of when I was growing up. I guess we used to leave such events to the Girl and Boy Scouts, churches, and families. Now, however, school-sponsored sleepover camps are a big part of the curriculum of many elementary and middle schools.

Although sleepovers are a familiar activity in our culture, you might be surprised to learn that many kids hit fifth grade (where sleepover camps usually begin) and have never slept away from home or have only slept over at the home of a relative. Moms and dads are understandably hesitant to place their kids in a situation that might be uncomfortable or unpleasant. The problem is, many of these camps are set up as part of the *curriculum.* Papers and projects are tied into the events of the camping trip. In fact, my kids went to a couple of "educational" camps which had instruction and completion of homework as part of the camp. I have seen 12-year-old sixth graders who were taller than mom sobbing piteously on mom's shoulder as a bus full of his classmates waited for him to board.

Some schools schedule a week-long camping trip during the first six weeks of school, in order to help the children "bond." (I swear this is true.) So if your kid misses out on the bonding experience because he is too terrified to leave home for a week, you have to worry about whether this will jeopardize his future social life in that classroom. How can you get your child to participate in the event without traumatizing his future development?

The answer is easy; you volunteer to be a chaperone. That way, your child can enjoy the camping experience with you in the next cabin over. Aah, but what about your job, your other children? If you can't arrange to be there yourself, how about sending a favorite aunt or uncle, a grandparent? Is there anyone in the family who can volunteer? (All volunteers are, of course, subject to any required volunteer paperwork and medical documentation.)

I have to admit I was somewhat taken aback when I heard that my sixth-grader was expected to go on a week-long early October camping trip with her new school. She had previously been to summer camp, as well as a three-day school camp at a marine institute the year before, so I didn't have to

PARTIES, PICNICS, & OFF-CAMPUS TRIPS

Camping in the Angeles National Forest

worry about her fears. I did worry about the fact that she knew no one in her class and about the fact that I couldn't go on the trip (chaperones had been selected the previous spring). I was lucky, though. One of the other mothers who went as a chaperone took my daughter under her wing.

The sleepover camp proved to be a very positive experience for my daughter. Located in the Angeles National Forest, it gave the children a week-long wilderness education, complete with nighttime hikes, cooperative living arrangements, and the usual singing and crafts. They even got rock-climbing practice by climbing to the top of the chapel.

The following year, my son's *fifth grade* went to a week-long October educational camp which is owned and operated by the school district. That was his *first* sleepover camp, but he was comforted by the fact that many of his friends since kindergarten were also attending and that parents were allowed a mid-week visit.

Camping with classmates: a chance to make new friends

By the way, most of these school sleepover camps are not free. The ones my children have attended run anywhere from $100 per child for the three-day island camping experience (which is subsidized by two years of candy drives run by *you-know-who*) to nearly $300 per child for the week-long event. The school district camp was free except for a nominal meal charge.

CHAPTER SEVEN

And don't forget, you will have to provide your child with camping gear to make these trips. Don't be surprised if you have to come up with another $100 or more to properly outfit him or her with good shoes, warm jackets, etc. If your child has been in the same school since day one, you probably have a good idea of what the school camp schedules are. If you are planning to change schools, it is wise to check with the new school before fall to see if any such events are pending. That way, you can prepare both your child and your budget for an extended school trip.

Camping Trip Gear

1. Sleeping bag
2. Pillow
3. Space blanket for extra warmth
4. Good walking shoes
5. 2 pairs of jeans
6. 2 pairs of shorts
7. 3 T-shirts
8. One warm sweatshirt
9. Windbreaker/rain poncho
10. 1-2 long-sleeved shirts
11. Underwear
12. Socks
13. Waist pack / water bottle
14. Warm socks
15. Toiletries
16. Notebook/pen
17. Pajamas
18. A heavy jacket
19. Sunblock
20. Hat
21. Important phone numbers
22. Disposable camera
23. Bathing suit
24. Towels

The camping experience can be an important part of your child's education. Particularly if they are born and raised in the city, the outdoor experience can be an introduction to a whole new way of life. They may be "on their own" (within a very protected setting) for the first time. They will usually be assigned housekeeping chores which they are expected to complete in a cooperative and cheerful manner. At many camps, children are taught about the delicate ecological balance between civilization and nature. They are often encouraged to conserve food by weighing the total food that kids left on their plates at the end of each day. Students may have their first sighting of new plants and animals and an opportunity to explore different terrain.

In a way, camping is a mini-introduction to the type of group living experience that many of our children will encounter if they go off to a live-in college. They will have to learn how to share living quarters with new roommates, eat in a dining hall that may not offer Mom's home cooking, and manage their own free time (albeit within a structured environment). Before sending my kids off to school camps, I was most worried that they would starve to death because they are such picky eaters. Instead, both children returned having tried (and liked) foods that they would

PARTIES, PICNICS, & OFF-CAMPUS TRIPS

An introduction to animals, up close and personal

never eat at home. My son got more homesick than did my daughter, but we didn't get any late-night calls to pick him up. He grew from the experience and has fond memories of it.

Since many of our children no longer go to neighborhood schools, their only experience with many of their friends is in school. A week at camp gives them the added level of friendship that is forged by out-of-school experience, including just plain playing together, staying up late telling stories, and being assigned to work and study teams. Kids who may not get along so well in school often find different and better ways to relate in a new setting. The stress of classroom competition is reduced or eliminated, and the kids can simply be kids having a fun time. If the children happen to learn despite themselves, well, so much the better.

Even if you feel hesitant about letting your child attend a week-long school-sponsored camping trip, try to overcome your own fears and encourage your child to go. Kids who were sobbing at the bus are often the ones who benefit the most from the experience. They come home with a new sense of independence and competence. No, they won't be less close to you, but they will be more confident about their abilities to face new situations. It's as good a time as any for you to practice letting go.

Class Trips

Camping and field trips held in grades K-7 prepare you for what could be a shocker (well, for me at least): the eighth grade class trip. Okay, maybe I'm jealous. I never had a class trip of any kind at any age. I had previously heard of senior class trips, but eighth grade? What a surprise.

My daughter transferred from a private to a public school for eighth grade. About two weeks into the semester, she came home with a document informing me that a meeting would be held that week for parents of students who wished to send their children on the Washington, D.C. – New York City class trip to be held that following April. Excuse me? We live in California.

CHAPTER SEVEN

Photo by Sierra Weir

Take time to relax and enjoy the view

Did they really expect me to send my then 13-year-old on a three- thousand mile one-week trip which included stays at two hotels in very large cities? They did. What's more, they weren't asking for parent volunteers, *and* the trip would cost $1,200. They didn't even have room for the entire class to attend. The trip was on a first-come, first-served basis. In other words, get your money in ASAP to ensure your child's spot on the trip.

My by-now-world-weary traveling daughter (who has logged more miles of vacation trips and camping expeditions than most adults) insisted that she be allowed to go. She begged ("What, you don't trust me?"), she pleaded ("Everyone is going."), she bargained ("I promise to keep my grades up!"). She even chipped in the down payment from her own savings. What could I say?

First, with help from Dad and the Grandparents, we budgeted for the trip. Then we made convenient monthly payments. When spending over $1,000 for a school trip, it is extremely advisable to throw in the extra fifty or sixty dollars to buy the trip cancellation insurance. That way, if something comes up (your kid has the flu, a family emergency, etc.), you are guaranteed a full return on your expenditure.

Next, we shopped. She had to have a fancy dress for dinner before the Broadway Show in New York City. She needed dozens of rolls of film and insisted on taking her very expensive 35mm camera. Her dad provided a cell phone, because the students were blocked from making long distance phone calls from the room (smart hotel), and she would have had to wait in line with 53 other kids to use the lobby pay phones. She needed shoes to match her dress, a haircut, a manicure, a good daypack to carry on the plane, plus all the various and sundry items that kids take on a week-long trip. And don't forget mad money! There went another three or four hundred dollars.

PARTIES, PICNICS, & OFF-CAMPUS TRIPS

Photo by Sierra Weir

Teachers from Dodson Gifted and High Ability Magnet Middle School enjoyed chaperoning the 8th Grade Class Trip to Washington, D.C., April 2001

After all the preparations were made and she was safely on the plane (a red-eye flight from LAX to Dulles), I went home and worried. I worried that she would leave her camera somewhere or that someone would steal it. I worried that she would wander away from her group (they were on a strict buddy system, but were allowed to "meet back at Point A" at a certain time). I worried that she would lose her cell phone, that the hotel would burn down, that she would be kidnapped, or that she would get sick, lonesome, or scared. I worried about everything a parent could possibly worry about. My imagination was on overtime. But I controlled myself, waiting patiently for her to call me every night, desperately trying to keep myself from micro-managing her trip. (Is your dress on a hanger? What did you eat? Where is your money?) Okay, so I didn't do such a great job on that end. But I *did* allow her to go, and she did come home in one piece.

Photo by Sierra Weir

Capitol Building, Washington, D.C.

She brought home dozens of beautiful photos, a raft of trip stories, and a new perspective on our nation's beautiful and stately capital, the workings of our government, and the vast difference between East Coast and West Coast cities. I'm glad I sent her. She has since used the photos in different school projects. Every little while, she

CHAPTER SEVEN

Your child will come home with amazing photos

informs me of something I didn't know about either city or about history and government. It was a tremendous learning opportunity for her, albeit a daunting "school project" for me!

Today's schools are not simply places where we send our kids to learn. Educational institutions design a learning environment for our children which includes both classroom and non-classroom instruction. I have covered a few of the different situations in which children are expected to leave the classroom, yet are still considered to be "in school." To a great extent, parents can participate in these off-site experiences. In doing so, we offer support and encouragement to both our kids and the schools. We also learn to mentor other parents and help allay their fears of sending their kids along on extended off-campus trips. The hardest part for me, even now, is the few hours before they are due home. I can manage to stay busy for most of the time my kids are away, but when I'm preparing to go pick one of them up from a trip, school-related or otherwise, all the "what-ifs" rise to taunt me. It's not till I see them coming down the boat ramp, or off of the bus or plane, looking strangely separate, walking a bit taller, seeming more confident, that I'm glad I was able to support this aspect of their learning experience.

Chapter Eight

How You Can Help Your Child

How to Think Up Project Ideas

When your kindergartner or first-grader comes home and says, "Mom (or Dad), can you help me make a stuffed animal or dress my favorite teddy bear or make a cardboard scale model of our house for class tomorrow?" you may feel a bit hesitant or even overwhelmed for a minute or two, but let's face it, *it's do-able.* So you gather up some boxes from the garage, some scissors, construction paper, and markers, rummage through your sewing box for fabric scraps and stuffing, then you get down to business. Your end product may be lopsided or a bit unstable, but your kid thinks you're a genius.

CHAPTER EIGHT

Photo by Sierra Weir

Dress a bear or make a stuffed butterfly

One thing your can be sure of is that the projects get more complex and demanding as your little one advances through elementary school. Instead of offering specific directions, Annie's teacher will produce an assignment that leaves the thinking to the student. For example, California fourth graders are usually charged with creating a model of a Spanish Mission or Native American dwelling or artifact. I assume that other states have some type of historical architecture or anthropological artifacts which more clearly represent their state history. From the time my daughter was in second grade and first noticed the fourth graders bringing their completed projects into school, she was anxious to get started on her mission project. I wasn't too worried about it. I figured we'd go to a model store and pick up a set, then spend a fun evening gluing and painting. *WRONG!* That was before I read the fine print, which clearly stated that the model must be constructed from scratch by the child, using ordinary items. The use of Styrofoam, plastic, or wooden models was strictly forbidden.

Deciding which California Mission to model was only half the fun. We pored over books and discussed materials for what seemed like forever. Finally, we settled on one that looked less complicated to build. Our buildings were squares and rectangles cut from foam, then covered in quick-drying plaster and painted. The roofs were made of folded cardboard covered in a dark red vinyl fabric that we glued on. The area outside the buildings was made from an authentic-looking sand/dirt type of product, the kind model railroaders

HOW YOU CAN HELP YOUR CHILD

use. We used plastic fences, horses, farmers, and Native Americans from a long forgotten set we found in the toy box. Everything was anchored to a piece of wood that was about three feet by two feet, one which I found out, as I carried the model into school for my daughter, was much too heavy to be easily carried.

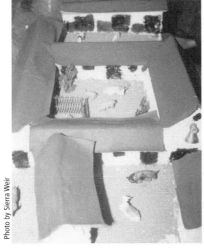
Photo by Sierra Weir

California Mission Model by Sierra Weir

From the mission project, I learned several things. One, start saving interesting pieces of cardboard to be used on my son's mission project. Use something lightweight as a base, e.g., Styrofoam, plastic, or light wood, stay away from plaster (it wasn't nearly as quick-drying as it said, at least not when applied to foam) and make sure the paint you use is not too runny (we found a new use for white-out).

Given all the difficulties of the mission project, it still wasn't as difficult as thinking up something out of the blue. Most of the time, the teacher has some idea of what he or she wants: a report on a state, for example. But within the report on the state, there may be a "special project" which is described only as "Develop a model or other educational display which informs the other students about your state." This is about as vague as a teacher could get and still be giving instruction. The worst part was, that section was worth 50 points, or about 25% of the project grade. Ignoring it was out of the question.

CHAPTER EIGHT

Photo by Sierra Weir

Indiana State Project

My daughter got the bright idea of making a brochure, "Ten Great Reasons to Visit Indiana" to go with her "Indiana A-Z" cards (see Chapter Two). She included pictures of Indiana historical sites, entertainment areas, products, famous people. This was a great idea, but not quite as easy as it sounds. At nine o'clock the night before the project was due, my daughter and I were still at Kinko's finishing the layout and lamination.

Your child won't always be able to think up an idea on his or her own, and you are the person most likely to be pumped for ideas. Be prepared. All you need is an open mind and a willingness to help. Here are a few places where I have guided my children to seek project ideas.

HOW YOU CAN HELP YOUR CHILD

Books

Books may seem like such an obvious place to look for information and ideas that you might wonder why I would even mention them. But until you have children raised in today's environment, you may not realize how unlikely a choice books will be for a child. This does not apply to those families who go to the library like clockwork each week; you know who you are. Everyone wants to rush to the Internet or find a video about the desired subject. But I'm old enough to like the solid heft of a good encyclopedia or other reference book in my hands. I love to wander among the library stacks, pulling out amazing out-of-print materials that may never show up on the Internet or anywhere else. You may have a difficult time convincing your child that books are still in vogue, but it's worth it.

Your child may be drawn only to the "Children's Books" section of the library, but don't forget to check the adult section as well. Many books designated as adult level reading may contain illustrative photos or diagrams that help your child develop his subject. Even before my son could read really well, he was totally capable of understanding, reviewing, and reproducing diagrams. Also, it is important to remember that not all books written for adults are particularly difficult to read or comprehend. Many children read far above their grade levels and can benefit from reviewing books that aren't necessarily labeled as recommended for children or young adults.

If you can't find what you are looking for in the main areas of the library, ask about special reference rooms. Many libraries also have ongoing sales of old books in rooms that may only be accessible at certain times or by appointment. Every month or so, our library also puts boxes of donated books on the front steps with a big sign that says "Free." For whatever reason, the library is unable to stock or sell those books. I have added some wonderful texts to my personal library from these castoffs, including college texts on biology and chemistry, high school literature anthologies, classic novels, and "how-to" books of all kinds. Don't forget to visit used bookstores for great buys on books, magazines, maps, and reference materials.

CHAPTER EIGHT

Magazines

Magazines are a bit less foreign to children as a source of information. If you're like me, and you can't bear to throw magazines away because you *might* get around to reading the back issues, or you fully intend to clip all those interesting articles for your file someday, then you have stacks and stacks of ready-made project fodder, your own mini-archive of current and not-so-current events. A few publications that can be found around my house include: *New Yorker, Atlantic Monthly, Newsweek, Reader's Digest, Audobon, National Geographic, Girl's Life, Ranger Rick, Highlights, Yankee Magazine,* and a few others. Okay, a few dozen.

It's amazing what you can glean from a magazine when your child goes into a panic because he or she remembered the project just after you bestowed your final goodnight kiss and were padding back to the living room to relax and browse through the newspaper. Not only can you find all manner of lettering and fabulous photos to cut and paste, you can also dig up articles that are focused and easily summarized or paraphrased for your child's consumption.

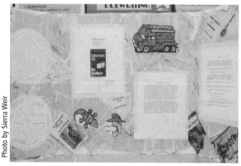

Photo by Sierra Weir

Magazine and newspaper illustrations used in "Character Wheel" **Fahrenheit 451** Book Report, by Michael Koger, Linda Velasco's 8th Grade English class, Dodson Gifted and High Ability Magnet Middle School, RPV, CA

These days, children are often, not always, asked to illustrate their paragraphs, book reports, and presentations. I've seen my children in tears many times because they believed "illustrate" meant they had to draw. Have your child check with his or her teacher on this. In my experience, when a teacher says "illustrate," that doesn't necessarily mean the child has to render his or her own interpretations. Many teachers are happy if the child produces a paper or project within the larger definition of "illustrate," i.e., *to clarify with photos or pictorial representations intended to elucidate or adorn.* In other words, grab your scissors and start cutting.

HOW YOU CAN HELP YOUR CHILD

The Internet

As I mentioned above, while the Internet is seen by the current generation as the answer to everyone's homework problems, my children and I have often been quite frustrated in our attempts to find information or to find complete and thorough information on a given subject. True, there are times when an entire report can be based on information gleaned from various educational or personal websites. But remember, the Internet is new; it will be an awfully long time before all the information that is available in libraries and books has been made fully Internet accessible. A more fundamental concern is the reliability of information published on the Web. The old saw about not believing everything you read is doubly true for information found online. Teaching children to question the validity of sources may be the most important lesson of a research project.

If you have a computer at home, then definitely use it as a starting place. It is an invaluable source for finding titles of books and articles that meet your needs. Many library catalogues can now be easily accessed from your home. You may be able to determine whether a library stocks a book and whether it is checked out. You can search the larger library system and place a hold on the book you want for delivery to your local library. If you are interested in buying a book, you can log on to Amazon.com or some of the larger bookstores' sites and simply order what you need for delivery to your home.

The Internet can also lead you to local or fairly close museums or special collections libraries that can provide more specific information for your topic. Instead of spending hours on the phone trying to organize an educational trip for your child's group, you can browse various websites for information on likely destinations. You can make reservations, order tickets, or, if a visit is out of the question, let your child view an interactive tour of the site.

CHAPTER EIGHT

The Great Outdoors

Depending on your geographic location, your child may have access to a wealth of project-friendly ideas and supplies literally right outside your door. If you live near the ocean, you can collect samples of shells, seaweed, driftwood, sand, or rocks to develop a three-dimensional display for a science project. Perhaps your child has a penchant for collecting things. How about helping little Sarah press a selection of wildflowers or tree leaves that she can then research and present as a science survey. If you live in the mountains, an illustration of how mountains are formed could be jazzed up with a selection of rocks found in your area. If mining is underway, you could take your child on an excursion to a mining site, to see exactly how the materials are extracted from the earth. Safety first, of course, but there are mines that offer trips down deep inside the earth for a first-hand look at the industry. Schools usually won't want the liability of such a field trip, but as a parent, you can do it. Only you know what is available in your own immediate area. Make sure you take advantage of your area to enhance your child's education.

Photo by Sierra Weir

Collect shells and driftwood for use in future projects and displays

Photo by Sierra Weir

Give your child a camera to catch nature's miracles

HOW YOU CAN HELP YOUR CHILD

Videos/DVDs

Our children have grown up with videos. They see them in school and at home, many times more than once, even more than is good for them. So why not throw an educational video into the mix? I have to admit, a couple of times when my daughter seemed disinclined to finish a book (or was unable to for one reason or another), I allowed her to get the video from the library and watch it so she would be able to write her report or pass her test. I know, some would say that was cheating, but the goal was that she process the story. If she couldn't or wouldn't read it for whatever reason, I thought it best that she get the information in whatever way was available. Often, she was disappointed in the film presentation, but this opened up a line of discussion about interpreting the written word and the function of imagination in reading.

Because of their early exposure to TV shows, today's students are well-suited to receiving information from videos. Libraries are usually well-stocked with historical and documentary videos about every conceivable subject. And don't underestimate the value of "The History Channel" or "Discover" or "Animal Planet." While a video shouldn't form the *entire* basis of a report or presentation, it can certainly be an added source of information.

Once your child has seen a few videos about various subjects, he or she may get creative and wish to make a video. This is an exceptionally good technique for your child who is giving an in-class report about his family history, his neighborhood, pets, friends, or for the child who wants to produce a play for a literature or history class.

CHAPTER EIGHT

Family History

At least once in every elementary school career, a child is asked to produce either a timeline of his own life or a family history. If you are somewhat organized and keep your family photos in some type of order, these types of projects can be a snap. For some of us, it can also be a learning experience, as we call our own parents and grandparents and ask for details of when and how we came to this country or that state. As you seek to help your child develop a sense of family history, you may inadvertently discover other topics for future projects. For example, in researching our family history for my daughter, I learned that those who came on the Mayflower had nothing on my family, who first settled in New France in the early 1600s. I also learned that my ancestors had intermarried with the Mohawks, one of the Iroquois tribes. There's a history project in the making.

Photo by Sierra Weir

Civil War Era Padlock

On my children's paternal grandmother's side, they learned of a famous artist; and on their paternal grandfather's side, a few inventors and some cowboys. They also learned that their grandmother's ancestor, C.C.A. Christianson, had been the official artist designated to document the Mormon crossing into Utah in 1846. As you delve into the family history, you may come up with manuscripts, photos, and interesting artifacts. When my daughter was assigned a Civil War project in eighth grade, she found no Union or Confederate soldiers in our family tree, but Grandma did come up with some authentic Civil War coins that she was willing to lend out to be included in the display.

HOW YOU CAN HELP YOUR CHILD

Ancestor Artist C.C.A. Christensen's Sugar Creek was borrowed from Grandma for History presentation

When it comes to family, my motto is "You'll never know if you don't ask." A little in-house research never hurts. Grandma might have an adventure or two that she has never told anyone. Maybe she didn't think it was relevant. Maybe no one ever inquired. Is Grandma an avid quilter? Perhaps she could be talked into doing a demonstration at the Harvest Festival or teaching a workshop to your daughter's third-grade class. Why not get Grandpa to utilize his engineering skills to assist your young techno-genius in building his science project?

Vacations

Vacations are a part of American life, whether it's a short jaunt to the mountains for a ski weekend or a three-week adventure in Hawaii. When you're single or without children, a vacation can be one long round of eating, sleeping, and entertainment. But, as all parents know, a vacation with children can sometimes be more work than play. One of the things we do to keep our kids happy on vacations is take them around to see different sites and absorb the local culture. This is where education comes in and where the smart parent keeps his or her eyes open for project ideas. Face it, sooner or later the kids will be back in school, bringing you their project dilemmas. Little Eddie comes home moaning, "Mom, I have to do a project on the desert ecosystem by next Friday." You, the brilliant and forward-think-

CHAPTER EIGHT

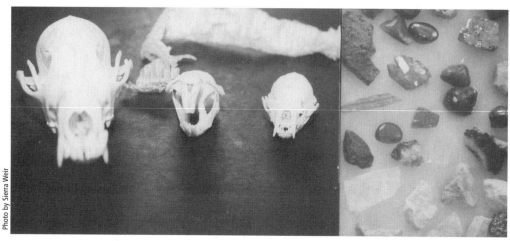

Look what we bought in Montana!

ing parent, go to your file and pull out the brochures and family photos from last year's visit to Palm Desert, where you just happened to take the children to every local museum and nature hike you could find. Congratulations, Mom, you're on the road to teaching your student how to plan ahead.

And don't start feeling guilty about "doing the project for your child." No, no, no. You simply facilitated a field trip to an educational site. Once your child reviews the photos and brochures, you'll be *amazed* at what he recalls about the trip, things that you didn't even notice. Whether it's a *what-I-did-on-my-summer-vacation* essay, a travel brochure, or a more in-depth research report, your child will not feel like he or she is starting from zero. On the contrary, he will adopt the air of the experienced journalist who only has to ask his assistant (you) for his backup materials in order to get down to business on his project.

HOW YOU CAN HELP YOUR CHILD

Local Museums and Other Attractions

Every region in the country has its own share of local history, which sometimes goes unnoticed until you need the information. I live near the coast in Southern California. Of course, I always knew there were plenty of beaches, where one could boat, swim, fish, and surf, but it wasn't until my kids entered school, and I started accompanying them on field trips, that I realized what an amazing number of other related attractions were situated on or near the coast. For example, there are several marine science museums and aquariums, where children can learn about how the coastline came about geologically, what types of sea creatures and fish inhabit our coastal area, how the marine ecosystem stays in balance, and what we can do to support the health of our oceans and coastal wetlands.

Photo by Greg Weir

Tour of the **Swift of Ipswitch**

There are also several maritime museums that educate the public regarding the history and practice of shipbuilding, sailing, and maritime life; wildlife stations that protect and help injured animals; whale-watching opportunities; and coastal hiking. There are even tall ships in our area which serve as summer camps for children who wish to learn how to sail. All this, within a few miles of my home.

Start early to become acquainted with all of the local learning opportunities in your area. If you live in an apartment, many small cities have community gardens, where you can rent a small plot for a nominal fee and teach your child to grow things. If you live in a more rural area, take your child to county and state fairs, enroll him in the 4-H program, or take him to the tractor museum in the next town. If you expose your child to many of the available local history sites, he or she will already have the makings of a brilliant idea when a project is assigned.

CHAPTER EIGHT

Many local airports have aviation museums attached to them, where your child can see aircraft of all sizes and shapes, including prototype vehicles, antiques, engines, control panels, equipment, and uniforms. And don't forget fire department museums, where pieces of old fire-fighting equipment are stored, generally as shiny as the day they were manufactured. Nothing sparks a child's imagination like being there, trying on the big yellow coats and red hats, sitting in the driver's seat, and making all the appropriate noises. Later, when Billy decides to compare the types of engines used in fire trucks versus trains, you can give yourself a self-satisfied pat on the back, knowing you helped foster his curiosity by exposing him to the realm of possibilities.

Local Organizations and Events

Another great place to seek inspiration for school projects is not far from your home. Most cities and towns, regardless of size, offer opportunities for children *and* adults to learn and expand their horizons. For example, if your child is interested in conducting some type of gardening experiment for a science project, you can take her to the nearest botanic garden and ask an expert for advice on what types of plants to use. If your child wants to do a report on horses, and you don't happen to have one, take him or her to a local stable to learn first-hand about what goes into raising and training horses. When we lived in Colorado Springs, there was a fabulous railroad club that met every Friday evening in a huge room where they were constantly adding to their elaborate train set-ups. My son learned much about constructing track layouts, model gauges, how to build little mock cities and landscapes, and it was virtually free.

Our local library often has special events designed to instruct children on various aspects of literature and music. They recently sponsored a series of demonstrations of different types of musical instruments. In the past, they have also presented puppet and mask-making events, as well as the usual storytelling and writing. Many libraries have "grandparent" study-buddy and tutoring programs. If your child is having trouble thinking up a story or project idea, why not stop by and talk to an older person whose experiences and ideas may be helpful?

HOW YOU CAN HELP YOUR CHILD

In our area, there are free whale-watching and harbor tours available during certain times of the year. Children's museums are another fabulous place for your child to gather information for future inspiration.

Project Supplies

I might as well admit it; I was one of those kids who waited anxiously all through the long, hot summers of my childhood for school to start up again in September. While many kids were swimming at the local pool, I was sharpening pencils and trying to decide if my old pencil pouch would last me another year. And amid the shouts and cheers of kids playing baseball at the park near my house, I drowsed on our porch swing, dreaming of the first day of school, wondering how the desks would be arranged, eagerly anticipating the snap of my ring binder as I deftly installed my looseleaf paper, longing for the pleasant scratch of my ballpoint pen as I wrote the perfect essays for my perfect teachers.

Okay, I was odd. But my love for school supplies has never dwindled and has probably rendered me the most well-equipped mom on the block when it comes to school projects. Some women swoon over dresses in department stores. If I have a couple of hours to spare, you can find me at Staples or Office Max, loading up my cart with reams of paper, report covers, and white-out from the clearance rack, or at Sam's Club, buying markers and highlighters by the gross and plastic sheet covers by the box. Paper clips, clamps of all sizes, Post-It strips for marking chapters, Elmer's glue in stick or liquid form, stapling supplies, construction paper – you name it, I want it. And I want it in bulk. I don't think I could ever have enough boxes of number four pencils, roller-ball pens in all colors, push pins, or fasteners. You get the picture.

CHAPTER EIGHT

Your At-Home School Project Supply Cupboard

Things to Buy

These days, at the beginning of the school year, most public and private schools send home a list of supplies that a student should keep in his or her desk or backpack at all times. Some lists are more extensive than others (e.g., they include a box of Kleenex to be delivered to the teacher or request that a child have his own stapler and three-hole punch). The list you receive is an excellent starting point for stocking your at-home school projects cupboard.

What cupboard, you ask? That's a good question. I'm talking about a special place in your home that you will designate as the project supply center. It could be a few shelves at the bottom of your student's closet or, if you have more than one child, a centrally-located cupboard or closet large enough to hold everything you might ever wish you had when your child needs it. In my house, most of the supplies are kept in my home office. There's something about those neatly stacked reams of colored paper, those little plastic drawer sets full of clips and pins and clamps, the boxes of envelopes, pens, and pencils, and the variously-sized posters and three-way boards that just make me feel happy.

If you don't have space for a designated cupboard, buy one of those sets of plastic drawers on wheels. They come in all sizes. We have one that is about four feet tall, just packed full of odds and ends that always come in handy for that last little detail.

The lower drawers are deep enough to hold paper, and the upper, more shallow drawers are perfect for pens, erasers, glue, etc. The main idea is to have a centralized location for most of your goodies. It will make your student feel secure to know that he or she has the necessary supplies to prepare a great project. I'm not saying you'll never need to go scouting for one thing or another, but the following list should lend a bit of serenity to your project preparation.

HOW YOU CAN HELP YOUR CHILD

1. **Paper, as much as possible, as many types as you can find.**
   a. College or wide-ruled looseleaf paper
   b. Construction paper
   c. Tracing paper
   d. Computer paper in various colors
   e. Card-stock paper
   f. Decorative paper
   g. Tissue paper
2. **Poster board, in whatever colors are available. (Look for the thick kind, that you can push tacks into.)**
3. **Three-way display boards for science projects**
4. **Poster paper that is more like light cardboard**
5. **Brown wrapping paper (in rolls)**
6. **Graph paper**
7. **Sketch pads, all sizes**
8. **Glue**
   a. Elmer's, aka, school glue (white and runny)
   b. Glitter glue – comes in colors, dries clear and glittery, like Elmer's
   c. Glue sticks (less messy, but sometimes too dry)
   d. Crazy Glue (sometimes necessary, but for use only with parental supervision, so the kitchen table doesn't end up glued to the project.)
   e. Fabric glues
9. **Staplers and staples**
   a. Very small ones, to carry in a backpack or keep in a desk
   b. Normal-sized, for stapling 1-10 pages
   c. Heavy-duty, for stapling longer documents
   d. Long-arm staplers, for binding mini-books
10. **Paper clips, all sizes and shapes**
11. **Clamps, all sizes and shapes**
12. **Report covers**
13. **Notebooks: 1/2" – 2" rings**
14. **Subject dividers**
15. **Post-It Notes, all colors and sizes**
16. **Heavy-duty two-hole punch or top-bound reports**
17. **Heavy-duty three-hole punch or side-bound reports**
18. **Notebook-size three-hole punch**
19. **Pencils, No. 4**
20. **Pencils, No. 2**
21. **Colored pencils**
22. **Markers, various sizes, as many colors as possible**
23. **Rubber bands, all sizes, colors, and thicknesses**
24. **Yarn**
25. **Crepe paper**
26. **Popsicle sticks**
27. **Pipe cleaners**
28. **Acrylic paints**
29. **Watercolor paints**
30. **Erasers**
31. **Pens (red, black, blue, green)**
32. **Colored gel pens for coloring (not for schoolwork)**
33. **Plastic sheet covers**
34. **Envelopes, all sizes and colors**
35. **Styrofoam balls, rings, squares, all sizes**
36. **Cotton balls, all colors and sizes**
37. **Balsa wood**
38. **Q-Tips**
39. **Toothpicks**
40. **Glitter, any color you can find**
41. **Stickers, all types and sizes**
42. **Crayons**
43. **Oil pastels (similar to crayons)**
44. **A large office calendar (to keep track of project due dates!)**
45. **Index cards, 3x5 and 5x8**
46. **Large rolls of white butcher's paper**
47. **Velcro strips or patches**
48. **Needles and thread**
49. **Buttons**
50. **Cotton stuffing**
51. **White-Out (which now comes in bottles, squeeze tubes shaped like pens, and as a tape that rolls on)**
52. **Rulers**
53. **Compasses**
54. **Protractor**
55. **A few disposable flash cameras**
56. **Quick-drying plaster**
57. **Printer ink cartridges**

CHAPTER EIGHT

58. Packages of plastic "eyes"
59. Sinew
60. String
61. Beads (all sizes, colors, materials]
62. Little bells
63. Origami paper
64. Clay or Playdough or directions for making same (see Appendix).
65. Butterfly or moth cocoon cages

66. Tape
    a. Scotch tape
    b. Masking tape
    c. Clear package tape
    d. Duct tape
    e. Two-sided tape
    f. Electrical tape
67. Felt (by the yard, in squares, or the new squares w/ sticky backs)
68. Paper plates and cups (holiday-themed)
69. Plastic knives, forks, spoons
70. Paper napkins
71. Sandwich-size plastic bags

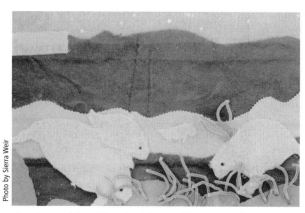

Pipe cleaners, felt, and fuzzy fabric jazz up this touchable Manatee poster

A saved ribbon and a class trip photo combined to make a unique cover design for this handmade book.

HOW YOU CAN HELP YOUR CHILD

Recycling Stuff into School Projects

Besides all the things you might buy to stock your cupboard (and the above list is probably incomplete), you will want to start saving certain items that you would otherwise toss. These are mostly everyday things that you would never think about putting to any use until the first time your child comes home and asks for one. So get a head-start *now* and be prepared *later* to have a stash and save policy in place.

1. Egg cartons
2. Cardboard rolls (all sizes, from toilet paper to paper towels to linoleum size)
3. Old greeting cards
4. Cylindrical containers such as oatmeal boxes, coffee cans, etc.
5. Brown paper grocery bags
6. Cardboard boxes (all sizes, shapes, and colors)
7. Cardboard packing, esp. if made into interesting shapes and textures
8. Styrofoam packing supports
9. Old pantyhose (make good stuffing in a pinch)
10. Any type of interesting container that came as part of packaging
11. A certain quantity of old newspapers (for protecting floors and tables, as well as for use in papier-maché projects)
12. Old postcards
13. Old stamps, particularly from foreign countries
14. Old clothes that might be worked into costumes or recycled as fabric
15. Doubles of current family photos; copies of antique family photos
16. Ribbons
17. Old socks (make great puppets, bracelets, or bean bags)
18. Old jewelry (can be recycled for decorations or as jewelry on figures)
19. Old hats, shoes, or boots
20. Old thread spool, esp. wooden ones if you can find them
21. Wooden boxes with sliding lids (the kind that wine bottles come in)
22. Fabric scraps
23. Old toys that can be reused in whole or part to build models or for use in demonstrations

CHAPTER EIGHT

Look Around Outside Your House

When you are through rummaging through the house for things to stock your project cupboard, take a walk around your neighborhood and local parks and see what else you can find. Since childhood, I have collected leaves and pressed them inside books. When you have enough different kinds (and colors, depending on the season), your student can make a little nature scrapbook for

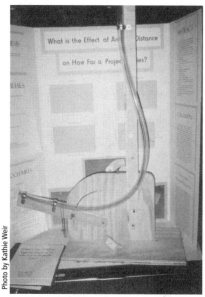

a science project. We have found some very exquisite-looking seed pods that, when spray-painted gold, made an excellent holiday decoration. Remember, if you're bothering to read this book, you're probably destined to be a room mother, so you will have to come up with classroom decorating ideas.

Pick up a fallen branch that can be stripped of bark, sanded, and cut into cylindrical slices. Find a friendly mom or dad to drill holes in the resulting disks and you can teach your child to do decoupage, perhaps to creatively illustrate a three-dimensional project or as a "demonstration" project to share with the class.

Photo by Kathie Weir

Science Project by Brendon Kerr, 7th Grade, Dodson Gifted High Ability Magnet Middle School, RPV, CA

HOW YOU CAN HELP YOUR CHILD

Here are some types of things that we regularly bring home from our walks and hikes:

1. Driftwood
2. Shells
3. Random pieces of interesting wood
4. Leaves
5. Seed pods
6. Pussy willow branches
7. Cattail reeds
8. Pine cones
9. Pretty rocks
10. Petrified bugs (I know, yuk)
11. Birds' nests and/or eggs (empty of course)
12. Butterfly or moth cocoons
13. Cornhusks from the garden (to dry and use to make cornhusk dolls)
14. Soil samples (for science projects)
15. Wildflowers

As a precaution, children should be instructed *never* to touch an unknown plant unless an adult is guiding them. Some wild plants can be poisonous or irritating, even to touch (e.g., poison oak). The same instruction should be given regarding bugs and animals. When my daughter was a toddler, she was stung by bees and wasps three times on her fingers because she would actually *pick them up* (she thought they were cute!). She was forever walking into preschool with some big black beetle-type thingie crawling up her arm or handling pill bugs and worms like they were her best friends. She has even been known to pick up snakes on the trail. And we have watched countless moths and butterflies hatch from cocoons after she brought the fuzzy little caterpiller home. So, for your own peace of mind, without scaring the child to death, teach him to have a healthy fear of unknown living things. Keep in mind, though, teachers love the students who bring in interesting examples of nature in action.

CHAPTER EIGHT

Where to Shop

Now that you've read my rather extensive lists of absolutely essential items to keep on hand for school projects, you are probably questioning your decision to have kids, or perhaps worrying that you will never be able both to pay a mortgage and to keep your kids in school supplies. Don't panic. This is the United States of America! We live in the land of warehouse and discount stores. Sooner or later, everything I mentioned (and I keep thinking of new things to add to the list as I write) is either on sale or in the clearance bin. You just have to plan ahead, buy ahead, and know where to shop.

Nothing makes me feel more in control of my child's educational success than standing at the checkout in a warehouse store, my cart piled high with bulk packages of tape (6 rolls plus dispenser), highlighters (12 for under $6.00), a couple of boxes of computer paper, a super package of report covers (bonus buy, 12 for the price of four in a regular store). Office supply stores are always an adventure. Be sure to check out the clearance bins first. The other day, I found clear plastic sheet covers on sale: 88¢ for 25. On the same rack, I found a knock-off of White-Out strips, also 88¢. It may seem indulgent, but it's worth stocking up when you realize you will eventually have to come back to that store and pay $4.88 for the same or a similar product. Sometimes, you find great deals where you least expected, such as in chain drug stores or department stores.

Never pass up the opportunity to buy in quantity. There is often a temptation to say to yourself, "I'm glad I saw that sale; I'll come back on Tuesday when I have more money." Let's just think about that statement. If *you* believe it's a great deal, you can pretty much bet that the next five or ten people coming through the store will have the same opinion, except that they will *buy* the items. In fact, if they're smart, they will buy their own share, plus yours. When you come back on Tuesday, there will be a few lonely folders lying about on nearly empty shelves. And you will have passed up a great opportunity to prepare yourself for the next great project. Remember, stocking the proper materials is half the battle. Don't think of stocking up as spending money. Think of it as *saving time*, your time. Just the other day, I *finally*

HOW YOU CAN HELP YOUR CHILD

found a three-inch ring-binder for my son. His school requires that he have one, and he had broken his a month earlier. For some reason, although those huge binders were everywhere when school started, I had to search through about eight stores to find one. Actually, not one, but three. I found three of the type of binder I needed in the clearance bin (where else?) marked down from $12.99 to $4.00. You'll never guess what I now have in my school projects cupboard. That's right, two extra 3-inch binders, just in case my little angel breaks another one before the year is up.

Right after a holiday is also the perfect time to stock up on holiday-themed paper plates, cups, napkins, etc., for those never-ending class parties that you will be asked to host. On November 1st, it may seem like next Halloween is a long way off, but just think how you will feel a year from now when you go to your cupboard and find a full supply of jack-o-lantern plates and cups for your second grader's party. And the post-holiday sale is a great opportunity to stock up on little gifts for your child's classmates. I know, not every mother wants to hand out 25 pencils with ghost erasers on top, but there are plenty of us who engage in that sort of behavior, at least while our kids are in the primary grades.

Just a few days ago, I was in a Goodwill store where they had an entire rack full of Halloween and Thanksgiving napkins, paper plates in two or three sizes, cups, paper table clothes, everything I ever wanted, and they were selling for about a buck a package. Imagine: 48 cake plates for a dollar! A mother of a kindergartener could have stocked up for her child's entire elementary school career. Let's face it; fads come and go, but Halloween and Thanksgiving motifs have basically remained the same since before we were born: pumpkins, ghosts, witches, black-orange-green for Halloween; and corn, turkeys, horns-o-plenty, leaves, gold-brown-tan-green for Thanksgiving.

Besides the holiday items, it's always good to stock up on regular paper plates and cups for those inevitable class picnics and school events for which you will be asked to donate items. If you get enough of a supply in ahead of time, you can tip off the teacher at the beginning of the year that she should ALWAYS put you down for paper supplies.

CHAPTER EIGHT

Warehouse Stores
1. Sam's Club
2. Costco

Office Supply Warehouse Stores
1. Office Max
2. Office Depot
3. Staples

Discount Department Stores
1. Target
2. Walmart
3. K-Mart
4. 99-Cent Store
5. Pic N' Save
6. Fabric and crafts stores

Retail Drugstore Chains
1. Rite-Aid
2. Sav-On

Thrift Stores
1. Salvation Army
2. Goodwill
3. Assistance League

Yard Sales, Garage Sales, Etc.

Another great standby for kids' parties is boxed juice. They last a few months and are often on sale, so grab them while they're cheap. Vacuum-packed snacks, such as individual servings of chips and crackers, also have a long shelf-life. Soft drinks for making punch and jars of salsa dip are also great standbys. Just check expiration dates every few weeks. If it looks like you're not going to need an item for an upcoming party, you can always use it in the kids' lunches or at a sleepover.

Of course, many of the stores I mention are in California, because that is where I live. You can probably make a list of the same types of stores in your shopping area. The main idea is to familiarize yourself with what is out there and then make a habit of scouting the various locations once or twice a month. Make a commitment to periodically invest a few bucks until your cupboard is so well-stocked that the school board is knocking on your door asking to borrow pencils. Earn a reputation in the neighborhood as the mom who always knows when the projects are due, what the assignment really says, and where to find the right materials. Become the mom that other moms call in a panic to ask if you have any staples, a three-hole punch, or a copy of the "scientific method."

I'm not saying I never pay full price for anything, but I will say it breaks my heart to do so. I am constantly on the lookout for interesting paper, eye-catching stickers, the close-out on scotch tape. What difference does it make if you don't use the stuff you bought for a couple of months? At some point, Junior will have a project and you will be organized and ready-to-go. Remember, for some projects, all you really need to do is provide the materials. Your child may have been carrying an idea around in his head for weeks. Support his genius with a fully-stocked supply cupboard.

HOW YOU CAN HELP YOUR CHILD

Execution

One of the most important aspects of a project is how it is put together. It should be secure and stable, well-constructed, and tidy-looking. As parents, we have the dilemma of either stepping back and letting the child do it completely (which can result in a mess) or finding a tactful way to guide the project without actually doing it. In the lower grades, neatness is a criteria, but not the most important aspect. At those levels, teachers simply want to see that the child can complete an assignment. But by the time middle school rolls around, teachers are looking for attention to detail, a sense of proportion and balance, and some real originality in design.

To Glue Or Not to Glue

Glue is fine if your child learns to use it correctly. Most schools no longer use those big jars of traditional library paste (you remember, the kind we used to eat). The runny white "school glue" (aka "Elmer's") works well, but is very easy to over-use, causing letters to smear and colors to run. Children have to be carefully tutored to gently squeeze dots of school glue onto the page, then spreading them into lines. Otherwise, the project quickly becomes soggy and unmanageable. The good news about school glue is that it dries clear, so even if the errant spots are dripped onto the front of the project, it won't show in the end.

Glue sticks are wonderful and usually fairly inexpensive. They can be safely transported in backpacks. The most common problems I've seen with glue sticks is that the child doesn't apply a thick enough coating on the paper or the stick is a bit dried out. Glue sticks also come in various sizes, from a bit larger than a Chapstick tube to fit smaller hands to fairly large tubes. I usually have glue sticks on hand at all times.

Glue guns are effective, but need more supervision, especially if they are being used by younger children. I like to use them to glue fabrics or pieces of cork, wood, Styrofoam, shells, etc. to boards or other display pieces.

CHAPTER EIGHT

Photo by Sierra Weir

The Hiding Place by Corrie ten Boom with John and Elizabeth Sherrill, Diorama from Linda Velasco's 8th Grade English class, Dodson Gifted and High Ability Middle Magnet School, RPV, CA

Crazy Glue is a miracle, but, as you know, can glue fingers to tables. We keep a tube of "Crazy Glue Remover" on hand, just in case. I don't recommend using Crazy Glue for your average paper and cardboard projects, but it is great for dioramas or displays in which you want objects that have a little weight to stay put (preferably permanently). For more information about different types of glue and how to use them, check out **www.thistothat.com**.

HOW YOU CAN HELP YOUR CHILD

Lettering

Photo by Sierra Weir

Magazine lettering used in collage

These days, teachers LOVE to see typed projects. Some teachers even request that students use 14-point font on papers, I'm assuming in an effort to save their eyesight. With the computer, your child can choose from dozens of different fonts and type-sizes which will make his or her project attractive and professional looking. However, if you don't have access to a computer at home, your child can still create interesting lettering to label a project. Starting with the basics, he or she can simply do it by hand. Many children are blessed with the ability to hand-letter their displays, posters, and labels, achieving an artistic effect with block lettering, calligraphy, or neat printing. To help your child achieve a consistent size and orientation of letters, you can use a very light (no. 4) pencil to draw nearly invisible sets of lines for him to follow.

If your child prefers not to hand-letter, he or she can browse magazines and find colorful and artistic lettering to cut out and glue to his or her board. Or he could cut out the letters from construction paper, sticky-backed felt, or any other type of decorative paper (e.g., foil wrapping paper) to make the letters stand out and add an aesthetic accent to the project.

CHAPTER EIGHT

Coaching vs. Doing

Every child needs to learn that even though Mom and Dad are willing to run all over town to purchase supplies, take him to the library, show him how to use the computer and Internet, hold the parts together until the glue sticks, and proofread his work, they are not going to do the entire project for him. Or even 50% of it. It's great to bond with your children, but when you and/or little Davie begin talking about "our project," a red flag should go up. With schools expecting so much from our children these days, it's very easy to get over-involved to the point that you are actually producing some of the work that your student is handing in. We walk a very fine line between coaching our children to get their own work done and actually doing it for them.

I'm not saying I've never felt like I was stepping over the line, particularly when my child has had to juggle four or five projects within the same 5-6 week period. On several occasions, I've had to step back and admit that I was investing too much of my own self-esteem in the project's outcome. From day one, I think parents should talk to their kids about how much time and effort they are willing to contribute to projects and homework. Then stick to your own guidelines. Some projects are so much fun and so creatively stimulating that it's hard not to want to do it all yourself. But you can't.

Your child must learn to rely on himself and his own inspiration to produce projects. Sometimes, that means your child's idea of what is a great project will conflict seriously with your own concept. You must bite your tongue, be as supportive and uncritical as possible, and urge her to discuss her ideas with her teacher. Other times, your kid will come up with an idea that will absolutely astound you. Either way, it's his project, his grade, and his education. Be available to help, but don't help so much that the child's input becomes unnecessary. Eventually, you want to hear what I've been hearing since my daughter entered ninth grade last fall. "I've got a project due three weeks from today, but I already know what I'm going to do and how I'm going to do it. I just need a ride to the library, some time on the Internet, and here's my list of supplies."

Chapter Nine

Computers and the Internet

About three years ago, my children and I were at a yard sale where someone was selling an old Remington manual typewriter. My kids were fascinated with this amazing machine. We just *had* to buy it. I spent twenty bucks on the typewriter and another fifty to have it reconditioned. For days, they had it out in the living room, trying to figure out all its features, impressed that it could type in both red *and* black. At the time, we had three working PCs in our home, and my children were both fully proficient with both mouse and keyboard. But they reacted to the typewriter as if it were the wave of the future. There was something about all those moving parts, the very effort involved in pushing the keys down, that made it an astonishing find.

CHAPTER NINE

I tell that story because we had one of those typewriters in my house when I was in high school. In college, I thought it was a big deal to get a portable typewriter. I typed other people's papers for extra cash and was able to get a work-study job on campus because my speed was a big sixty words a minute. Now I live in a house where everyone has his or her own personal computer, along with Internet service and printers.

When it came to computer technology, I went kicking and screaming into the Twenty-First Century. My daughter was born in 1987. At that time, I was aware of computers, even knew that I would soon have to confront learning to use one, but hadn't yet made the transition from my Selectric Typewriter to a PC. It was only when I realized that I wasn't going back to the office after she was born and simultaneously got an offer to work at home, provided I had a PC, that I made the plunge. There I sat, baby screaming in the background, tears running down my face, trying to learn WordStar (a now-obsolete program). It seemed as soon as I mastered one program, another took its place. Everything I learned was a result of some emergency. A new client needed a different format. Macros were being implemented. I needed a faster printer. It was probably three years before I felt even remotely comfortable using the computer. Even so, I mainly used it as a glorified type-writer for many years.

I'm embarrassed to admit that I didn't even approach using the Internet until 1999, when everyone began asking, "Do you have an e-mail address?" Since then, my entire way of doing business and living life has changed. I now rely on the Internet to keep in contact with people, and it is often my first choice to find information or answers to questions. I do my work on the computer and send it in via e-mail instead of commuting thousands of miles. My children's schools require them to do Internet research. They need various programs to complete homework assignments, including Excel, Access, MSWord, Corel, Paintbox, and others that I probably don't know about. From a manual typewriter to the high-speed Internet service of today, all in one lifetime: if I did it, so can you.

COMPUTERS & THE INTERNET

Kids and Computers

If your kids are anything like mine, they first saw a computer screen when they were barely old enough to stand up, and they began playing computer games as soon as they could muster the hand-eye coordination to make their fingers press the keys. Unlike their mom, both of my kids were easily manipulating a mouse before they entered kindergarten. Not that I was very happy about it, you understand. I never wanted them to spend any time in front of a computer screen, even if they were playing educational games. But they would come into my home office and see me sitting there, hitting the keys, and see things happening on the screen (even letters appearing was interesting to them). Then they would ask if they could try it. Of course, I said yes.

They saw their father playing some of the early computer games and that was even more interesting than what mom was doing. The next thing you know, they're being familiarized with computers and computer games in pre-school and kindergarten, at the homes of friends and families, and, yes, even in their own home. I think we began buying "educational" computer games in the early 1990s. My kids played the "Oregon Trail" and "Rabbit Reader" games, "Tetris," "Math Blaster," and all the rest. By age ten or so, they were busily working to decode Mavis Beacon's touch-typing instructions and learning WordPerfect. In fact, I had worked on WordPerfect 5.1 for so long that my 9-year-old son had to instruct me on WordPerfect 6.1. That was the first program I had to become familiar with that utilized the mouse in favor of the keyboard. I won't even tell you how long it took for me to develop the hand-eye coordination required to make the cursor go where I wanted it to on the screen. For some reason, I couldn't get the hang of which way to move the mouse to correspondingly move the cursor. I suffered lots of frustration over that issue. It's absolutely humiliating to see your grade school kids do so easily what takes major effort for you to accomplish

CHAPTER NINE

Schools and Computers

Within the last decade, schools began including computer instruction as part of the weekly curriculum. Depending on the school district, our kids began to have access to computer labs as well as computers in the classroom. The proceeds from many of our elementary school fundraisers went directly for the purchase of computers. Various foundations and the computer companies themselves often made donations or gave discounts to enable us to purchase four or five terminals at a time. Computer labs grew from four or five terminals with three to four kids being instructed at each one to rows and rows of shiny new PCs and Macs, one child per terminal.

In many of today's classrooms, there are at least three or four computer terminals in the back, which teachers utilize during "group rotations." They are equipped with headphones and programs that can coach, drill, and test your child in a number of areas, including math, spelling, reading comprehension, and social studies. Kids are given a password to access their personal files. They then complete various worksheets and tests on the computer. The teacher can monitor their progress by accessing her own computer program, which records how much work each student has completed.

Most elementary school children complete at least one or two computer projects per year. They learn to do research via programs such as Encarta, Collier's Encyclopedia, and other reference programs. They use drawing programs to illustrate stories that they write using the word processing feature. Children learn to keep their work on a disk that stays in the teacher's desk until they go back for their next computer lab visit. Sometimes, they bring those disks home from school to work on a project. If your child shows up with a disk, the very first thing you should do is save whatever is on it to your hard drive, then make another disk, just to be safe. Too often, we've had the disappearing disk dilemma or the "disk-won't-open-when-it's-time-to-print disaster." Save yourself! Schools are striving to get enough volunteers to keep the computer lab open after school hours for kids to use to catch up on homework or learn to use the keyboard.

COMPUTERS & THE INTERNET

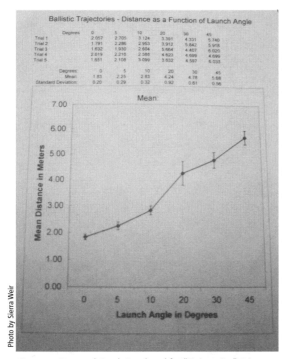

Computer Data and Graph Developed for "Trajectories" Science Project, by Brett Weir

Photo by Sierra Weir

In middle schools, children can take a computer class as an entire semester elective. There, they learn how to operate the computer and its many programs for maximum productivity. My daughter already knew how to touch-type before she took her eighth-grade computer class. But she did learn to use various programs, including Access, a database for storing comparative information or lists (e.g., addresses) which can be manipulated to produce graphs, tables, or selective groupings, MSWord, currently the most-used word processing program, and Paintbrush, a program that allows her to select and/or create, manipulate, and crop images.

She also learned to use the Power Point program, which organizes information, e.g., a book report or research presentation, then delivers it in a series of revolving images, much like our old slide shows, but in a much more professional manner. Power Point is used by many types of professionals to make sales and other office presentations.

CHAPTER NINE

Photo by Sierra Weir

Photo by Sierra Weir

Is the Main Character a Hero?

I do not believe that the main character in *Kindertransport*, Olga Drucker, is a hero. A heroic character is often an extraordinarily courageous individual who performs selfless deeds or makes personal sacrifices. Olga performs no heroic deeds, or acts in any way, but the people who care for her, do. They are willing to possibly risk their lives for a Jewish girl, who is in danger of being murdered by the Nazis and Hitler. They also try their best to take care of Olga and care deeply care for her. Olga however just keeps being transferred around, and never really gets to appreciate any one household. The children that Olga meets are also very friendly towards her. They are willing to treat her as any other kid, and learn to like her like their best friend. Because of this, I view the many people that helped Olga as heroes, while I do not consider Olga to be one herself.

CD Cover and Screens from Power Point "Character Wheel" Book Report, "The Books and Films of Kindertransport" by Nic Jordan, Linda Velasco's 8th Grade English class, Dodson Gifted & High Ability Magnet, RPV, CA

Photo by Sierra Weir

The Books and Films of Kindertransport

Photo by Sierra Weir

Kristallnacht: November 9, 1938

Many teachers are now giving students the option of developing a book report or other informational assignment using a Power Point presentation. Teachers like taking home a collection of disks instead of hauling posters and notebooks around. They pop the disks in their PCs at home, then sit back for an enjoyable review of each student's work.

COMPUTERS & THE INTERNET

Computers in Education

Those of us who live and work with computers may not understand how limited the child is who doesn't have access to a computer. Some teachers take for granted that *everyone* has a computer or access to one. This isn't true. Although the cost of computers is a fraction of what it was a few years ago, it is still likely that more kids come from homes that don't have computers than from homes that do.

No one can deny the importance of computers in our world. With each passing day, we increasingly rely on computers to perform the most basic of tasks. Many teachers now keep all their grades on computer files. They regularly send home computer printouts of your child's up-to-the-minute progress reports. My daughter's science teacher once lost all of her students' grade files. She knew they were still in the computer, but couldn't figure out where she had stored them. She offered 50 extra credit points to whichever student could find them for her. Only a few were brave enough to try, but it was my daughter who found them and got the 50 points.

The schools are trying valiantly to provide students with the computer training and practice they will need to compete in today's academic environment. I don't know of anyone who thinks a typewriter would suffice for students. From about the fourth grade forward, teachers ask for typed work. Some teachers request that it be typed in a 14-point font, which is fairly large, but probably saves their eyes. If you have ever had to wade through a few stacks of kids' handwritten homework, you will understand why teachers would rather look at neat, crisp, and clear typed letters.

Photo by Sierra Weir

Computer Printout of Student's Grades

CHAPTER NINE

I have a suspicion that computers are part of the cause for the decline in students' handwriting. Many children who grow up with access to computers learn to type before they ever hold a pen or pencil. Typing is fun; it makes things appear and disappear on the computer screen. It makes the computer screen change colors, play music, and tell you if you got the right answer. What is the child's incentive to laboriously form letters on a page? I've even seen the problem in my own handwriting. My hand muscles are now accustomed to typing instead of writing. When I try to write in cursive, I find that I leave out letters or literally struggle to form them. My handwriting is sloppier than it used to be, and my hand tires very easily. I also can't write fast enough to keep up with my thoughts. In contrast, I can type over 100 words a minute and then correct many errors with the spell check feature.

Speaking of the spell check feature: some teachers will allow students to type their papers on computers, provided they *don't* use the spell check feature. That is because they want the student to learn to spell without relying on the computer. Remember, spell check doesn't pick up spelling errors where the student substitutes homophones for each other, e.g., if your child used the word "road" when she meant "rode," the spell checker won't spot that mistake. Both "road" and "rode" are correct spellings. Spell check primarily picks up on typographical errors, unusual names, or technical words. It doesn't know what your child *meant* to say. Spelling is still an important skill that students must learn.

Computer Tips
1. Teach your child the keyboard.
2. Install educational software.
3. Take advantage of the Internet.
4. Install Internet filtering and monitoring software.
5. Spell check, but don't forget spelling.

COMPUTERS & THE INTERNET

Affordable Equipment

A couple of years ago, my son bought a vintage early 80s Apple computer, in the box, complete with lots of software, a manual, and a ton of instructional materials. He purchased it as a collector's item, and approached it with the same awe as he had the Remington manual typewriter. Tucked into the good-as-new box was a full-page newspaper advertisement, featuring that very Apple PC for the amazing sale price of $1,200. Back then, computers were out of the range of most of our pocketbooks. Fortunately, today you can go to a used computer store and buy your child a decent basic computer, sold with all the necessary software that a student needs to complete schoolwork and projects, for under $300. Brand new inkjet color printers are sold for under $100; they print everything.

While the equipment that one finds in used computer stores is, well, *used*, most of it comes with some type of guarantee. Many parents can afford to buy top-of-the-line computer equipment for their kids. If you can do that, more power to you. However, giving kids access to computers (and eventually, the Internet) in your home is not an all-or-nothing proposition. You can set up a very good, workable PC terminal in his room for not much money. Whether you also decide to grant him access to the Internet is up to you. Making that decision requires some knowledge or what the Internet can and cannot do for your child's education.

CHAPTER NINE

Freedom of Expression: Formatting Fun on Computers

One thing I do love about kids using computers is that they are able to add design and formatting touches to their papers, personalizing their work by utilizing the many software programs that enhance their creativity. Some teachers want *only* text. Others allow a certain amount of self-expression, such as borders or photos on the title page of a paper or illustrations throughout.

My daughter has turned in many poems that were printed in a stylized format which enhanced the tone or subject matter of the work. Children are often called upon to design travel brochures for ancient destinations, such as Egypt, as part of their coursework. With all of the formatting tools available on the Internet, a child can turn out a three-column, two-sided brochure with photos, multiple fonts, and colored borders, fresh from the printer, all ready to be folded.

Printing headings and captions for posters is also a snap. The child simply chooses from dozens of font styles, then selects the desired font size. No more struggling with markers, trying to keep lines straight, or correcting giant mistakes. If your child has a gift for illustration, the paintbrush option is also very helpful. Maps, charts, and borders can be added anywhere in the paper.

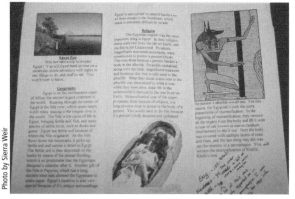

Egypt Travel Brochure by Brett Weir, Kevin Allen's 6th Grade Social Studies class, Dodson Gifted & High Ability Magnet, RPV, CA

Photo by Sierra Weir

Computers make headings and captions a snap. Book report by Brett Weir, also from Allen's class

Photo by Sierra Weir

COMPUTERS & THE INTERNET

Internet Use in Schools

Like many parents, I was hesitant to support the installation of Internet access in our schools. I experienced all the same trepidations and angst about kids wandering onto websites where they didn't belong and being exposed to all manner of adult material that would steal their innocence and taint their sensibilities. After several years of monitoring what goes on in my children's schools, and with the installation of various Internet Filtering and Monitoring Software (such as Net Nanny, Software4Parents, and similar services), I am fairly comfortable that my children are gaining the benefits of using the Internet without suffering too much of the downside.

When my daughter took her computer class as an elective, the students were allowed to surf the Net for research purposes *if* they had all their work done for that day. She was unable to check her e-mail, because they had the webmail and chat room sites blocked. In the average computer lab setting, even if such sites weren't blocked, it would be nearly impossible for students to go too far astray. The seats are fairly close together and most teachers walk among the class, monitoring the students while they offer assistance. For these reasons, I really don't spend much time worrying that the Internet is having a bad effect on my kids in that sense.

Staying in Touch with Teachers and Homework

One very positive aspect of the Internet which I have found helpful is the availability of e-mail contact with the teachers, administration, and the homework hotline. Many teachers now freely give out their e-mail addresses as a way of helping parents keep in touch. This is especially helpful to parents who work and may not always be able to find time to call during school hours. Plus it saves the teachers the time of tracking down parents by phone. We all know how many notes sent home by teachers to parents are mysteriously lost each year. One of my daughter's junior high teachers routinely sent out the week's assignments each Monday to any parent who gave her an e-mail address. It was so easy to ask, "Did you do the worksheet for Chapter 9 yet?" rather than "Do you have any science homework?"

CHAPTER NINE

Many schools now have their own websites, where teachers can post homework assignments each day or week. Each teacher has an identifying code for each class. Parents no longer have to listen to "I forgot to write down my assignment," "I don't have the number of anyone in my class to call for the assignment," or "I was absent, so I don't have to do it." At the beginning of the school year, you simply ask your child's teacher or teachers for the various Internet homework websites and/or their e-mail addresses and you will have a much greater sense of control over the homework situation for the rest of the year.

Internet Research

In many ways, Internet research is an amazing time-saver. The student simply logs onto a search engine (such as **google.com**, **dogpile.com**, **discover.com**, etc.), then types the name or subject about which he needs information. Like magic, a number of web sites appear which may or may not have the information you are seeking. The student reviews the lists that come up. If thousands of choices come up, you should suggest that your child refine his search by adding more detail to the original request. Please be aware that if you haven't installed the appropriate software to safeguard your child's access to certain materials, you may be unpleasantly surprised. The most innocuous search request can sometimes retrieve the most amazing selections. For example, I was astonished to see what was available when I searched Google for "pop-up books."

Once your child has retrieved a list of possible research sites, it may take awhile to narrow down which selections are actually on-topic for the search. One thing you learn is how many people have the same name! Another thing is how many different items that come up will lead you to the exact same website. Your child may spend a few hours sifting through all the possible sources of information about his subject to come up with at least a few that will support his research needs.

Sometimes we rely too heavily on the Internet, expecting it to have every bit of information ever printed about anything. The truth is, the Internet sometimes has nothing or next to nothing about certain subjects. Or it appears to have a lot, but it was all written by only one or two people or groups. The Internet is a wonderful starting place, but may end up being a waste of time. If your child can't find anything at all and the teacher is insisting that his bibliography include at

COMPUTERS & THE INTERNET

Towards Media Literacy

Ilene Raymond, author of **A Parent's Guide to the Internet**, writes that "by the time kids reach middle school, chances are good most of their information will come from the Web. For this reason, kids need to know how to critically evaluate information and how to judge what information fits their needs."

To that end, Ilene offers several questions kids should ask about the information they find online:

- Does the site cover the topic comprehensively and accurately?
- Are the links well-chosen? Are they up-to-date?
- How current is the information on the site? When was the site last updated?
- Can you get better information from another source (including non-Internet sources)?
- Who is responsible for the site? What are their credentials? Have they cited their sources? What is the domain: **.edu, .gov, or .com**?
- Can you find bias on the site?

least three Internet sites, it's time to talk to the teacher. Many, many times, the teacher has a list of on-point websites which simply aren't showing up on your child's search.

Be sure to ask at your local library how to log on to their electronic card catalogue from home. That way, you can teach your child to initiate searches for needed materials from your home. If your local library doesn't have what he needs, he can place holds on books from other branch libraries. When his books arrive at your local library, he will be notified via phone or postcard. Voila! Everything he needs will be waiting for him at the library, and you only had to make one trip.

Schoolwork for Sale

As noted elsewhere in this book, the biggest and worst mistake your student can make is plagiarizing the work of others. Unfortunately, the Internet has become a flourishing profit center for people who don't necessarily adhere to the same standards and ethics as we would like to teach our children. Before you allow your child to use the Internet for research purposes, make sure that he or she understands what plagiarism is and how it can hurt him, even if he doesn't get caught. It may be possible to block some of the "papers-for-sale" sites via some of the filtering and monitoring software. The least you can do is review your child's final drafts to make sure that the writing sounds like it came from *your kid*. If you have time, you might go over his sources to verify that he truly relayed the information in his own words.

CHAPTER NINE

Project Props

Another thing that parents should be aware of is that a number of the websites that seem to be responsive to a request for information are simply places to buy things. This may be okay, if you or your child is looking to buy something in relation to a project. This happened to us recently. My son was doing his science project on "Ballistic Trajectories – Distance as a Function of Launch Angle." He wanted to test his hypothesis using a model ballista (a medieval weapon, somewhat like a giant crossbow).

After a rather exhaustive search through local model stores, we learned that ballista model kits are few and far between. He began searching the Internet, in hopes of finding either a more distant source or a model ballista that someone else had made and was willing to sell. He found tons of photos and diagrams of ballistas, even plans to make one. However, most of the plans and diagrams involved making *fairly large* and *working* ballistas. We soon realized that it was unlikely that he was going to spend a year or two building a ballista large enough to skewer soldiers at 300 yards. Nor was he likely to be allowed into today's zero-tolerance schools with a smaller working model of a weapon that was actually capable of shooting miniature spears (the old "put-your-eye-out" admonition).

He spent a couple of days e-mailing everyone who had an e-mail address on any ballista-related website. Several people answered with advice about where to find ballista model kits. Many of those who wrote were part of a Medieval Warfare discussion group. Finally, our search led to a model manufacturer in New Jersey who sold the tiniest non-working metal model of a ballista for a mere $34.00 (postage and handling included). I shudder to think of what we would have had to go through to find this model without the aid of the Internet. And finding so many people who were willing to write to us, simply because we requested information, was really inspiring.

The Internet should be considered as just one of many resources available to your children. It is imperfect and, at times, overrated. However, it is also valuable if used correctly.

Chapter Ten

Important Concepts for Children (and Parents) to Take Home

Early Lessons for Academic Success

Elementary and middle schools are the training grounds for your children's future educational pursuits. As students progress through the grades, teachers build on information and skills in the hopes that students will acquire a foundation of learning which they will utilize as they encounter more complex and demanding subjects in high school and college. Ask any child what he or she is studying in school and you will hear the names of subjects, e.g., math, social studies, English, spelling, etc. Children focus on the obvious. They don't realize that they are also being taught other concepts and skills that will prepare them, not only for further education, but for their adult lives and careers. Parents must contemplate the big picture.

CHAPTER TEN

As we support and reinforce our children's mastery of facts and skills, we also have the opportunity to enhance their achievement by helping them to absorb the fundamental building blocks of academic success. Simply telling your child to "finish his homework" or "pay attention in class" is never enough. We must also be prepared to educate our children regarding the ethical and practical concepts that make the difference between so-so performance and true academic achievement. These concepts can be summed up as follows: the importance of following directions and doing one's own work; the wisdom of asking questions; methods for preparing a neat and complete product; the use of design and formatting techniques to enhance text; the art of giving and receiving constructive criticism; managing one's time to meet deadlines; and the development of people skills for surviving group projects. If our children are to succeed in school, careers, and life, they need a solid foundation of performance guidelines.

Don't be fooled into thinking that you can put off teaching your child some of these concepts until they are "old enough to understand" or "doing more difficult work." Most kindergartens, which used to resemble glorified play days, are now geared to jump start your child's education in a big way. Many school systems expect that your child will have had a year or two of preschool before entering kindergarten. If he or she isn't already familiar with the dos and don'ts of social interaction and doesn't have at least a passing acquaintance with his colors, letters, and numbers, he or she will be seriously behind the curve. In fact, many kindergarten teachers with whom I have interacted (either as a mom or substitute teacher) have lamented the fact that most kindergartens are currently following a first-grade curriculum.

Don't misunderstand me. I am not a big supporter of accelerated learning. I think it puts a lot of stress on many children, even has a burn-out effect on some, particularly those children who don't turn five years old until the late October deadline. Every parent has to decide which educational environment is right for their children and when to start their children's schooling. This book isn't meant to provide information regarding those decisions. I am simply bringing to parents' attention the expectations and requirements that their children will be facing when they begin their education.

IMPORTANT CONCEPTS

Parents, prepare yourselves. Kindergarten is where your child will first become familiar with homework, neatness, deadlines, grades, group interactions (not necessarily projects), criticism, and competition. It is the beginning of their indoctrination into the rules and regulations of academia.

The Purpose of Teachers

One of the best things you can and should teach your child about school is that it is a *safe* place where everyone wants to help the children do well. This is not to say that children are always going to click with their teachers (or vice versa). We've all had at least one teacher who scared us half to death and probably impaired the learning process in some way. After having been teacher's pet every year since kindergarten, I was quite astonished to be put into a sixth grade class in a new school where my teacher just plain didn't like me. Until that year, I would waltz into a class, calm and self-assured that my academic record and reputation as a very helpful girl would earn me my designated spot as the teacher's right hand. I think it took me until November of that year to figure out that it didn't matter what I did or said, how hard I studied, or how many times I erased the board, this teacher just wasn't interested in granting me the favored status that I had come to expect. A rude awakening, indeed. It wasn't until college that I again encountered a personality conflict of such magnitude.

We all know of at least one child that never got along with even one teacher in his elementary or middle school career. Until high school, my daughter seemed to annoy and/or alienate at least every other teacher she ever had. Some children are afraid of teachers and other authority figures in their lives. They may grow up with a persecution complex that they end up working out on the boss. Some teachers are disliked by everyone, including other teachers. Notwithstanding these extreme (but well-known) examples and the inevitability of personalities, it is a pretty sure thing that most teachers will do whatever possible to enhance the educational experience of every child in her class.

CHAPTER TEN

Parents should do likewise by promoting the basic idea that the teacher is there to help and that school is the place to make mistakes. *That's right!* Because if you never make a mistake, you'll never learn. Make it okay for your kids to not get a perfect grade or even fail a test once in awhile. This will give you an opportunity to teach your child how to recover from his mistakes, but more importantly, it will teach him to view the teacher as someone who is there not merely to hand down proclamations and judgments on his intelligence in the form of grades, but to facilitate his learning by continuously helping him develop strategies to process new information.

Once your child understands the purpose of teachers, classrooms, and tests, his fears and anxieties will diminish, allowing him to take advantage of the opportunities to learn that are provided free of charge in our educational system. One sure way to help your child readjust his perception of the teacher's purpose and goals is to readjust your own. Many parents carry over their own fear of teachers into adulthood and pass it on to their own children. One only has to look around on Back-to-School or Open House nights to see how few parents are truly involved with their children's education. Perhaps they carry bad memories of their own educational experience or feel as if the teacher will judge them poorly because of their own child's school performance. Regardless of what thoughts pass through your mind when your little one gets his parent-teacher conference notice, you must form a relationship with his teacher.

IMPORTANT CONCEPTS

Setting a Good Example

Clearly, the best way to develop a great relationship with your child's teacher is to volunteer in the classroom or offer to help out by preparing classroom materials in the school workroom or at home. If you can't do that, make sure to introduce yourself to the teacher early in the year, offer to help in whatever way you can, and keep the teacher updated about any special problems your child is having with school or homework or outside of school (e.g., a new baby, family moves, etc).

Always use positive words and tones when speaking of your child's teacher. If your child brings home an assignment, but doesn't understand something about it, model how to ask for information. Meet your child after school, then take her back to the classroom and ask for a few minutes of the teacher's time. Having tried various approaches myself, I find the best opener is, "Lilly and I are having a problem understanding what you want in question seven." This is much more effective than, "This is a really stupid question. Why did you ask it?"

When teachers hand out an assignment, they almost invariably ask if anyone has any questions. Don't be surprised if the teacher asks your child why she didn't ask about her assignment at that time. Your child might say, "I didn't hear you" or "I don't know," but they will seldom tell the truth: "I didn't want to look stupid." Many, many, many children (and lots of adults) are simply terrified to ask a question for fear of being ridiculed by their classmates. How many of us have sat in a class, not wanting to raise our hands, then breathing a sigh of relief when someone else asked the same question. Learning is asking.

I have always told my children, "There is no such thing as a *dumb* question." Even if everyone else in the room knows the answer, you still need to ask the question if *you* don't know the answer. I also tell them that most teachers prefer that you ask *before* you do the assignment. It saves them the time of deducting points and giving the project or paper a lower grade. Teachers want students to succeed. I try to impress on my children the idea

CHAPTER TEN

that teachers are there to facilitate their learning, to forward their progress, and to help them over stumbling blocks. Of course, it is best if our kids learn to ask the questions themselves, but I don't see anything wrong with intervening if necessary.

I was helping my children ask questions on assignments and seek mediation for group project disputes right through eighth grade. Eventually, the frequency of my assistance was diminished because my children had seen me handle things enough times to be able to do it themselves. But if the parents don't teach the child how to interact with authority figures and elicit correct information, then who will?

Other Basics

This isn't a standard helping-with-homework book, but I would like to bring up the obvious for a moment. One of the most effective means of helping your child cope with the many assignments, projects, and papers he or she will be required to produce in his academic career is to make sure he has a quiet, well-lit, organized space in which to keep his supplies and complete his assignments. This doesn't mean that some kids won't always prefer to do their homework in an impossibly uncomfortable posture in the middle of the living room floor or at the kitchen table while you are trying to prepare dinner. However, a kid's desk can at least be a place to stack books, papers, pencils, and other necessary items, a centralized meeting ground for wayward backpacks, paper clips, rulers, and other supplies.

In this age of multi-tasking and overworked parents, and children who need an appointment book to keep their schedules straight, setting a nightly time to complete homework is nearly impossible. I know. But you can *try*. For instance, all homework must be done by 7:00 p.m. I don't know about your kids, but by the time mine get home from a six- or seven-hour day at school, all they want is a snack and some quiet time. Sending them to their desks to immediately do more schoolwork just seems cruel. Then there are the endless sports practices, music and dance lessons, cub scout meetings, bike-riding, and doctor appointments. What's a parent to do?

IMPORTANT CONCEPTS

My kids have solved some of their homework time problems by learning to read and write while being shuttled around town for various reasons after school. I bought them each a lap board to use as a mini-desk. (When will someone in the automobile industry think of putting airline tray tables on the backs of car seats?) Of course, doing one's homework in the car precludes accomplishing much in the way of Internet research or exceptionally neat papers, but they do manage to get a fair amount of math and science worksheets completed in the car. We've even managed to do homework on planes and in hotel rooms while on weekend vacations. Not recommended, but it has been done. As long as my kids are doing well in school (grades at B or above in our house), my general rule is "finish your homework before you go to bed." If they need my help, they know where to find me.

Following Directions

Most teachers will tell you that getting students to follow directions is among the most difficult educational challenges. One of my favorite exercises involves handing out a list of items that the students have to complete within fifteen minutes. The first two items direct the student to write his or her name and the date. Item three instructs the child to read all of the questions before answering any of them. As the students continue the assignment, many moaning and groaning about how stupid it is or how they don't have enough time to finish it, they eventually reach the last numbered item, which instructs them to not do any items after the third one. However, since most of them didn't follow the explicit directions in item three, which was to read all of the items, they made a lot of extra work for themselves.

The obvious lesson of that exercise is clear: follow directions. Children, as well as adults, have a difficult time following directions. How many times has your child come to you whining that he doesn't know how to do the math or science homework? He has a set of questions in front of him, but swears he doesn't know how or where to get the answers. Usually, if we go back to the beginning of the chapter and actually read it (or re-read it, if

CHAPTER TEN

necessary), the answers to his questions are right there, in black and white. Particularly in math, kids seem to resist going back to the model instructions and applying the indicated procedure to the problems at hand.

A number of teachers I interviewed identified the assignment of projects as one method of teaching children to follow directions. A project may consist of many steps that must be undertaken in a certain sequence. There may be interim deadlines and points awarded for partial completion of project segments. Coordinating and accomplishing the various steps of a project help a child stay focused without being overwhelmed. In the classroom, "staying on task" is one of the big items of education. It means that the child can go from point A to point B to point C without being distracted by himself or others and with a full knowledge of how those points relate to one another. Completing a project, whether it is self-generated at home or progressively worked on at school, requires the student to stay on task over a period of weeks or a couple of months.

When my daughter was in second or third grade, her teacher told us that we could enhance what she was trying to teach them in terms of their recall of tasks by asking them to retrieve items in the grocery store. In other words, give your child a string of little chores, e.g., "Do you see the freezer with the ice cream? I want you to walk over there, open it, and get me a quart of chocolate, then bring it back to the cart." She said to start by instructing the child to do a sequence of 2-3 things, then progress to more. Of course, we all have to keep a very close eye on our children. Unless your child is over 12 years old, I wouldn't send him over a couple of aisles in the grocery store to find something. But an eleven or twelve-year-old is capable of helping you shop. Think of it: two birds with one stone – you get help in the grocery store while training your kid to follow directions.

The ability to follow directions is an invaluable tool that we all use every time we learn something. If you coach your child to read, reread, and faithfully follow all directions received in school, the teachers will bless you, and your child will be that much better prepared for both school and life.

IMPORTANT CONCEPTS

Neatness

Having corrected my share of homework and in-class papers from students of all ages, I have to say that neatness goes a long way with me. Few children have perfectly readable printing or handwriting, and there are graduated standards of neatness that should be applied to children of different ages. However, it will be in your child's best interests if you continue to stress the importance of presenting tidy and organized work.

Schools help children to learn to write neatly by providing the wide-lined paper with a dotted line between every two solid lines. The purpose of using that paper is to help the child keep the parts of letters separate. The stems of "bs" and "ds" reach all the way to the top of the top solid line. The tails of "ps" and "qs" extend below the bottom solid line. The round parts of all four of those letters are enclosed between the bottom solid line and the center dotted line. While your child is learning to print and, later, write in cursive style, buy lots of that type of paper and let him practice making his letters at home. Also, for the sake of consistency, make sure he does all of his assignments on the same paper.

When your fourth or fifth grader graduates to regular looseleaf paper, buy the wide-ruled style until he learns to correctly space his words. Luckily, looseleaf comes with its own nice red margin down the left side. Encourage your child to use it. On the right side, there should also be some type of ending margin. Kids need to learn to think before they write. You can help by encouraging your child to look at the space left at the end of the line before deciding to write the next word. Is there really room there to write an 8-letter word? Or will it end up scrunched up or down the side of the paper in the right margin. In about seventh or eighth grade, students switch to the narrower college-ruled paper.

What about typed papers? With the advent of computers and their growing availability in schools, we are seeing a transition by many schools to asking for typed rather than handwritten work. This would be fine, except that, during tests, children must produce the good old handwritten essay. My son

CHAPTER TEN

ran up against the handwriting/typing issue just this year. All through elementary school, his printing and cursive writing were readable, but it took him so long to handwrite anything that his teachers and I agreed that it was best to let him type up his work. Which he did, with prolific gusto. His seventh-grade English teacher stopped him short by demanding that he handwrite all of his assigned essays, book reports, etc. She had a good reason. All of her seventh-grade students had to complete a mid-year "Performance Assessment Test" that involved handwriting an essay within a specified time period. These essays form the basis of the district's evaluation of the student's writing proficiency. Needless to say, he has spent a large part of this school year learning to write faster.

Another way you can help is by getting your child a nice, soft, efficient eraser. I have nothing against the erasers on the ends of pencils, but these days, they seem to be of a lower quality than they used to be. Or perhaps kids are just in a bigger hurry. I don't know. What I do know is that kids have a bad habit of either crossing out mistakes and leaving a big black blob on the paper, erasing with a bad eraser that leaves red or black streaks on the page, or erasing with the end of a pencil where an eraser should be, with the result of tearing the page because the little metal eraser holder is what contacts the page. Believe me, no teacher wants to see a paper full of black streaks and blobs and little wrinkled tears.

I don't know if I was the only one surprised to learn that the current generation of children believes it is okay to use a pen to do math homework. Who started this bizarre practice? I would think that only the most secure genius would be so arrogant. After all, isn't math all about erasing mistakes? Granted, erasable pens are all the rage, but they aren't always as erasable as one would like and, again, that nasty worn-out eraser issue keeps surfacing. Please, encourage your kids to use pencils for their math homework.

Last, but not least, the use of whiteout is not only permitted, it is encouraged. In fact, whiteout appears on the lists of school supplies that kids are asked to keep in their backpacks. I agree that whiteout is a wonderful substance, but children should learn to use it sparingly and as a last resort. Who wants to see a paper with lumps of white stuff here and there that has had words literally carved into it? Most pens don't do well when writing over whiteout, and pencils don't

IMPORTANT CONCEPTS

work at all. A student who has learned to think before writing, or who engages in writing a rough draft or two before doing his final version is much preferable than a student who seems to have a lifetime supply of whiteout at his disposal.

The neatness rule also applies to your child's preparation of displays and posters for projects. Poster boards should be crisp and clean looking, not bent and wrinkled. My son's sixth-grade teacher was always sending his students home with 12x17 poster paper for their projects. The only problem was, by the time my son got done rolling it up and stuffing it in his backpack, it was virtually unusable. So I learned to keep a stock of that type of paper on hand. To make sure it gets back to school in one piece, try laminating it. I know, it costs a lot, but it's worth it.

You may have to help your younger child with cutting – they simply cannot manipulate scissors around some edges. Computers are a godsend for making large font lettering for posters and display signs, but gluing them on straight is beyond the skills of many children. Speaking of glue, be sure to teach your child that less is more when it comes to glue. There is nothing messier than too much glue that penetrates the paper and makes colors and letters run or leaks around the edges of the glued item.

On the other hand, it is equally important that you be willing to let a second-grade project look like a second-grade project. The teacher isn't expecting your seven-year-old to produce a professional-quality exhibit. Parents who help their children soon learn that there is a delicate balance between the messy "I-didn't-spend-any-time-on-this-project" look and the naturally whimsical delivery of a child. By the time my son started kindergarten, rumors were still circulating around our school about a certain child who had routinely brought in seriously overdone projects. I never met the child or the mother, but she had apparently been the cause of a lot of eye-rolling among teachers and parents alike.

Steps to Scholastic Success

1. **Follow directions.**
2. **Keep it neat.**
3. **Use interesting designs and formats.**
4. **Do your own work.**
5. **Give and receive criticism with grace.**
6. **Meet your deadlines.**
7. **Ask questions.**
8. **Bond with the teacher.**

CHAPTER TEN

Design

Neatness and design almost seem like two sides of the same coin. A well-designed and executed project would certainly be neatly presented. However, a project can be neat but not necessarily eye-catching in design. In fact, two projects may have the same basic content, but the one that is more creatively designed may earn the higher grade. That may not seem fair, but we have to face the fact that we are all subject to the persuasions of color, texture, form, and style. If you don't believe that, just look around at what sells in our culture. Advertisers know that they can charge twice as much for the same product if it is sold in an interesting package. In a way, you must teach your child to think of his schoolwork as an advertisement about himself.

You may shrink from the thought of teaching design concepts to your child, protesting that you know nothing about the subject. But you do! You designed your wardrobe. You decorated your home. You instinctively know what works and what doesn't. Start with color. I usually encourage my children to stick with three or four background colors in any project. Royal blue, purple, fuschia, and pale blue are four that I like. If your child selects three of those colors and wants to use orange for the fourth, he's probably on the wrong track. If he insists on using orange, re-do the entire palette. (I have to admit, though, except for Halloween, it's *very* difficult to use orange to good effect.)

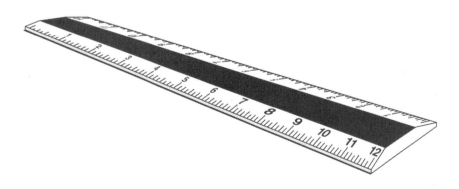

IMPORTANT CONCEPTS

Try to encourage a sense of symmetry in the design of the poster or display by balancing the colors. For example, if you use royal blue in the upper right corner, also use it in the upper left. If you are including printed materials, keep the text to a minimum and use a font size that is readable from a reasonable distance. If you use photos or magazine pictures, make sure they are adequately spaced and placed on a background color that complements them. Encourage your child to do a complete layout of the poster *before* any gluing, taping, or stapling begins. A word to the wise: for a major project, I always use the thick polyfoam board or three-way heavy cardboard posters because it is fairly easy to open the stapler and staple everything to them. Some boards are even thick enough to use thumbtacks or push pins. They cost a bit more, but hold up better and can be recycled into subsequent projects.

CHAPTER TEN

Plagiarism

Plagiarism: it's a teacher's worst nightmare and a student's biggest mistake. From the primary grades forward, your child will be regularly informed that teachers expect them to do their own work. Yes, their parents and older siblings may help. Yes, they may rely on traditional sources of information, such as books, museums, brochures, websites, and videos to obtain knowledge about a subject. But they must never, never reproduce the writings of another person word-for-word and pass them off as original work. That is called plagiarism. And it is strictly forbidden at all levels of academic writing.

Given that our children are being asked to write research reports at ever earlier grade levels, it may be difficult to clarify to your child what exactly constitutes plagiarism. Telling a fifth grader to "just say it in your own words" seems simple enough, but once he or she has read something, the child may not be able to clearly distinguish between his or her own words and those words in the book. Therefore, it is important that you guide your child by reviewing his paper and backtracking to his sources, so you will be able to help him see if and where he crossed the line.

Explain to your child that, whenever he wishes to directly quote or paraphrase the words of another writer, he must explicitly attribute those writings to that person, either within the text or in a footnote. The same is true if a person's ideas, theories, or opinions are used, even if not quoted verbatim. If a student is presenting other types of information, such as graphs, tables, or compiled statistics which do not reflect his own work, he must give the originator of that material proper credit for it.

Information which is considered "common knowledge" need not be attributed to anyone. An example of common knowledge would be "Television was invented in the middle of the Twentieth Century." This is a commonly-known fact that need not be attributed to any source. In contrast, study the statement "Scientists have found a direct correlation between the advent of the television set and the decline in the health of Americans of all ages." This

IMPORTANT CONCEPTS

is clearly an opinion that an elementary or middle-school child probably wouldn't have come up with on his own. Therefore, it should not appear in a research paper without an accompanying identification of its author or authors.

Since most research papers assigned to children under high school age focus on gathering information (versus coming up with original theories that are in part based on or in conflict with existing information), it is extremely important that your child be able to paraphrase information without reproducing it in exact form. Some children try to get away with substituting a few synonyms in the text of another's work or changing sentences around a bit. That doesn't fly, either. I agree that it often seems virtually impossible to reword information in any meaningful way. That is why we use quotes.

Sometimes, it helps to have your child just tell you about his topic of research, at the dinner table, while riding in the car, or while out for a walk. Ask questions. Make her explain her thinking. Then point out to her that she simply needs to write it as she is telling it. My daughter used to get stalled whenever she had a paper to write. When she was in fifth grade, I had the bright idea of having her tape record herself as she looked in a mirror and talked about the report. Then she played it back and typed it herself. For some reason, she couldn't get the information out directly from her brain to the page. But she had no problem talking about it and taping it.

Teachers do everything possible to impress upon students the importance of doing their own work. They hope that, by the time the student reaches college, they will have developed a practice of relying on their own efforts to write papers. Unfortunately, there are many in the world who seem to be moving in the opposite direction. Some of the worst offenders can be found on the Internet; companies buy and sell research papers as if they were school lunches. Sooner or later, your child will probably be exposed to the temptation to point and click his way to a ready-made paper. Now is the time to teach him that plagiarism is *never* acceptable, even if no one, including the teacher, ever finds out. He will still have to live with the fact that he stole another person's ideas and passed them off as his own for a grade.

CHAPTER TEN

Deadlines

When I was a college student, one of the rites of passage involved "pulling an all-nighter," i.e., staying up all night to cram for a final or write a paper that was due the next morning. I'm sure we all believed that the professors couldn't tell the difference between the papers that students had been diligently working on for weeks and those that had been finished within minutes of the class session that morning. Those were the days. However, I am now much too old to stay up all night doing *anything*, much less writing a paper or preparing a project. So I have worked long and hard to help my children understand and work within deadlines.

A deadline is the absolute last date on which a teacher will accept an assignment. Whether it is the daily or weekly homework or a large project, most teachers have a cutoff date after which the only possible grade is zero. In the primary grades, deadlines are rather loose. An assignment might be due on Tuesday, but if it is delivered to the "late box" within a certain time limit (usually about a week), the teacher accepts it as if it had been on time. As the child progresses through the grades, the deadline system becomes more severely enforced. As late as sixth grade, my son's math and science teacher was bending over backwards to help him make up assignments. He had this habit of doing them and then "forgetting" to hand them in. That teacher was a saint. Now that he is in seventh grade, he has had to learn the hard way that if it isn't in on time, it's not accepted.

Many teachers are now utilizing the "homework packet" system. The children are given a set of assignments on Monday, all of which are due on Friday. Depending on the grade and the teacher, these packets may include one or more math worksheets for the student to complete each night, perhaps some spelling or vocabulary words, and a social studies or English paragraph to write. My son's first grade teacher really went all out with the homework packets. They were as thick as a book and included "Must Do Assignments," "Suggested Assignments," and "If You Have More Time Assignments." She was a true optimist.

IMPORTANT CONCEPTS

Perhaps you have one of those rare children who feels compelled to finish the entire homework packet each night. If so, you probably won't have much trouble teaching that kid about deadlines. This advice is for those of us with children who say on Monday, "But it's not *due* until Friday, Mom!" Sit down with your child on Monday afternoon and decide which worksheets he will do on which days. If Wednesday is a busy school night, e.g., soccer practice, music lessons, cub scout meetings, then suggest that he do a little extra work on Monday and Tuesday so that Wednesday will be free. Never leave it all until Thursday night.

Teachers generally design school papers and projects with built-in interim deadlines. In other words, they divide the work into smaller sections and give deadlines for each section. For example, your child may be asked to turn in the subject of his topic on a certain date, the bibliographical sources he has located about one week later, an outline within a week or so after that, etc. If a student follows the prescribed time line, the work will be done in an orderly manner and a final paper or project will be completed on schedule. By incorporating the interim deadlines, teachers are giving children a hidden lesson in time management. They know that by the time the student enters high school or college, the handholding is over. Assignments state the topic parameters and indicate that the paper or project is due on a particular date, period. Any further arrangements, including questions about acceptable topics or scope of project, etc., are the student's responsibility. If all goes well, the student will recall his successful actions in preparing past papers and projects and will automatically repeat them, setting up his own timeline and interim deadlines. Or he may have to pull a few all-nighters himself before he figures out that the best results come from slow and steady progress and proper planning.

The interesting thing about deadlines is that they never go away. In adulthood, we are faced with deadlines in our careers and personal lives, and of course, we become the monitors of our children's deadlines as they grow up. Each year, we fight the tax deadline, the camp application deadline, the job search deadline, the expense report deadline. Life is like that. School gives your children the perfect opportunity to accustom themselves to handling

CHAPTER TEN

the stress of deadlines. You get to act as coach, secretary, chauffeur, assistant, and audience to your kids' progress in handling the large and small deadlines of life. Before you know it, they are adults, calling to make sure you sent your taxes in on time.

Giving and Receiving Criticism

One of the more sobering lessons a child has to learn is that the teacher's job is to help him become a better student. Sometimes, becoming a better student means changing bad habits, improving attitudes, or just plain working with more attention to detail. It is the teacher's duty to deliver those judgments and recommend remedies, mostly in the form of grades and comments on papers or projects. Children, especially those in the primary grades, are used to the total and unconditional love and praise of parents, who think *anything* their child does is spectacular, magnificent, and incredibly precocious. When kids start school, they often look to the teacher as a part-time parent who will pick up where mom and dad left off.

While it's true that teachers are often adored and looked up to with awe by students, the teacher has been trained to treat her students equally and to judge them based on the academic and developmental standards handed down by the local district. In other words, teacher is there to *help* your child, along with the other 20-25 students in the room. Teacher is a source of praise and security, encouragement and direction. But he or she is paid first of all to teach, not to coddle.

When your child brings home a paper with a lot of red marks or a "B" instead of an "A," he may take it personally, exclaiming that the teacher likes Billy better than him because she gave Billy an "A." Your job is to explain to your child the difference between the teacher's personal feelings and her job responsibilities. "Of course the teacher likes both of you, but maybe Billy made fewer mistakes than you did. The teacher has to be honest and give you the grade you earned." This is the time to review the paper and try to make sure your child understands what he or she missed and why.

IMPORTANT CONCEPTS

The first one or two or five times your child gets a bad grade from a teacher, she won't believe that the teacher is unbiased. After all, every single drawing she ever did is still on the refrigerator at home or at Grandma's house. Why doesn't the teacher adore everything she does? Just keep explaining that the teacher's job is to point out your mistakes and help you to not make them the next time. If your child does better in one subject than another, you can pull out his "A" grades and show him that the teacher will always give good grades if the work is correct. The trick is to help him understand that the grade the teacher gives him is an impartial evaluation of how well he did on tests, papers, and in class discussions.

I do not mean to imply that there will never be an instance where your child just plain doesn't get along with the teacher. Personalities happen; sometimes your kid is just in the wrong place at the wrong time. If you have done everything possible to facilitate a relationship between your child and the teacher and you still feel that your child is being treated or graded unfairly by that teacher, you always have the option to change classes or schools. But you should only do something so drastic in the presence of clear evidence. You don't want your child to get the idea that leaving an uncomfortable situation is always a good solution. Sometimes, the child just has to get over the fact that he is now in a group, no longer the center of attention, and that the teacher's efforts to be fair to everyone may impinge on his ability to do exactly as he wants.

If you think getting criticism from the teacher is a difficult pill for most kids to swallow, wait until your child comes home with his first "peer evaluation" sheet. Many school districts have adopted a practice whereby your child's work is being judged by the other students in the class. I know my daughter had many a sleepless night in fourth and fifth grades, not because she had to present the project, but because the other kids were going to "grade" it. She came home in tears a few times after her peer evaluation devolved into an all-out attack on her ideas, her costume, or the way her hair was fixed that day. In other words, most ten and eleven-year-olds aren't really ready to give unbiased and helpful criticism to their classmates. This came as no big surprise to me.

CHAPTER TEN

In every classroom where the peer evaluation procedure has been implemented, I have expressed my sincere doubts to the teachers about the effectiveness and advisability of this "learning tool." Most teachers I talked to admit that the criticism can get brutal and unproductive, but believe that there is some merit to teaching the kids early on to give and receive criticism. They also have assured me that the child's final grade on the project is really not affected by the other students' viewpoints.

As a survivor of many writing workshops, I know it never really gets easy to receive criticism from peers. But I have learned that there are better and worse ways to give criticism. I teach my children the standard procedure: always start out with something good, no matter how difficult it is to find. For example, "I love the topic you picked" or "Your colors are perfect." When you get to the negatives, only offer suggestions, not commands. "I'd like to see more pictures of trains and buses" is better than "Why did you leave this part of the poster all blank?" You get the idea. If nothing else, by learning to give less stinging and more constructive criticism, your child will be setting a good example for others.

As your child matures, he will come to view the teacher more as a mentor than a pseudo parent. And he will begin to understand that the teacher's job is to train his brain for increasingly more complex academic pursuits, not to baby him and falsely build up his ego. The art of giving good and honest criticism is a skill that teachers develop primarily to assist the student's progress, but also to model the procedure so that students will grow up to be excellent teachers, coworkers, and bosses themselves. It's another one of those academic extras that are woven into the daily texture of learning, but which are so important to our children's future success.

Appendices

Appendix A – Project Assignments

Appendix B – Stuff You Can Make At Home

Appendix C – Glossary

APPENDIX A

Science Report (Third Grade)

Predators

You are to choose an animal that is a predator. You will research, or gather information about this animal. Below is a list of the minimum information that you will need to complete this assignment. You should use dictionaries, encyclopedias, picture books, and the Internet to help you gather information.

Animal Predators Notebooks

1. Name of Animal:

2. Animal Family:

3. Scientific Name:

4. Habitat:

5. Typical diet:

6. Average life span:

7. Weight:

8. What physical features and characteristics does this animal use to kill its prey?

9. How does this animal hunt? In packs or by itself?

10. What are two interesting facts about this animal?

11. What animals are predators of your animal?

12. Is this animal an endangered animal?

The format and content of this project were created and provided by Jeffrey Clay, 3rd Grade Teacher at White Point Elementary School, San Pedro, CA

PROJECT ASSIGNMENTS

Diversity Unit Projects (Fourth Grade)

I. PROJECTS

Having studied the list of project choices, decide which ones you will do. Be sure you have selected one from each category.

II. GOALS

Select a goal for each project you decide to do. It will help you focus on the task. Here are some possible goals:

–to solve a problem: plan, design, construct

–to locate information

–to communicate information

–to think creatively

–to work cooperatively

–to show persistence

–others?

III. PROCEDURE

–Complete a planning sheet for each project

–Follow each plan

–Decide which projects you want to submit for a grade and for which subject area: Social Studies, Science, Math, Writing, Reading, or Art.

–Mark one project for each category:

•best work

•hardest assignment

•easiest assignment

•most creative work

•most enjoyable assignment

•assignment from which most was learned

–Arrange a conference to discuss work with the teacher.

The format and content of this project were created and provided by Eunice Morita, 4th Grade Teacher at White Point Elementary School, San Pedro, CA

APPENDIX A

Diversity Unit Projects continued...

Diversity Unit Projects

Select one project from each of the following categories. Use texts, encyclopedias, historical atlases, or other references to help you locate information.

I. MAP

A. The route of the Spanish missionaries and the location of the missions built in Alta California.

B. The main routes used by travelers to reach California during the Gold Rush.

C. Any historical map of California during the 1700's or 1800's. May be based on the journey of a fictional character.

II. DIAGRAM OR MODEL

A. A typical California mission, pueblo, or presidio (Mission System)

B. A typical California rancho

C. A typical California gold mining camp

D. A tool or form of transportation unique to these times

III. ORAL PRESENTATION

Imagine that you are making a Career Day presentation. Introduce yourself. Tell why you chose your job. Tell what you do on your job. Explain what training or skills are needed. Describe a typical day in your life.

A. vaquera or vaquero

B. padre or mission Indian

C. gold miner

D. a specific historical figure

IV. LITERATURE

READING CONFERENCE ON

A. Carlotta

B. Patty Reed's Doll

C. John Henry

BOOK REPORT

A. Biography

B. Historical Fiction

PROJECT ASSIGNMENTS

Diversity Unit Projects continued...

V. WRITING

A. A LETTER HOME:

You have immigrated to California, having left your family behind. You have had many new experiences and adventures to write about. Write a letter to describe your journey to California. What new things have you seen? What have you enjoyed? What hardships and dangers have you faced? Were your plans and preparations satisfactory? What would you do the same or differently? What advice would you give to your family for their journey to meet you?

B. BIOGRAPHICAL SKETCHES:

Immigrants to California made valuable contributions. Select 5 from the list and describe in 3-5 sentences who s/he was and for what s/he is known.

C. BIOGRAPHY:

Write a short biography about one of your relatives who immigrated to the U.S. or CA. Include: important dates, names of specific places, family members, where the person lived, why the person came to the U.S. or California, jobs held, and interesting things the person did. (If the person is deceased, tell date and cause of death.)

D. HISTORICAL FICTION:

Write another episode in the adventures of one of the fictional characters you have read about. Think about how your story will start. Decide what the main event will be and how you will end the story.

VI. MATH APPLICATIONS

A. Explain the economy of the Rancho, Mission System, or Gold Camps. How was money earned? What type of money was used? What was it spent on? What did things cost? Explain the concept of supply and demand.

B. List examples of how concepts of measurement were important during these times. Use facts about weight, distance, area, time, temperature, populations, etc. Think of 5-10.

VII. SCIENCE APPLICATIONS

A. Explain the importance of weather conditions for those taking one of the three routes to California. Tell why timing of departures was so important.

B. Explain the importance of particular plants and/or animals to the lives of the people living on Ranchos, Missions, Trappers, and Overland travelers.

C. Invent an item that would have made living in one of these time periods more comfortable or convenient. Diagram or describe its parts and construction. Explain how it would work. Explain its benefits. If you like, make a poster to advertise it.

California Mission Model by Sierra Weir

Photo by Sierra Weir

APPENDIX A

Diversity Unit Projects continued...

READING LIST: DIVERSITY

BIOGRAPHY – Choose any of the following subjects:

Gaspar de PORTOLA	Jedediah SMITH
Juan Bautista de ANZA	Kit CARSON
Junipero SERRA	John BIDWELL
Juan CRESPI	John BARTLESON
Pedro FAGES	Ezekial MERRITT
Jose de GALVEZ	Robert STOCKTON
Fermin LAUSEN	Mariano Guadalupe VALLEJO
Francisco PALON	John C. FREMONT
Pio PICO	Stephen W. KEARNEY
Manuel VICTORIA	John SUTTER
Conception ARGUELLO	John MARSHALL
Helen Hunt JACKSON	Joaquin MURIETTA
DONNER PARTY	Sam BRANNAN
Levi STRAUSS	Lotta CRABTREE
Peter H. BURNETT	JUANITA

HISTORICAL FICTION

Zia, Scott O'Dell	*Carlota*, Scott O'Dell
Search The Wild Shore, J. Montgomery	*3 Stalks Of Corn*, Leo Politi
Song Of The Swallows, Leo Politi	*The Secret Valley*, Clyde Bulla
Riding The Pony Express, Clyde Bulla	*Coarse Gold Gulch*, M. Gertwaite
By The Great Horn Spoon, Sid Fleishman	*The Golden Venture*, Jane Flory
The Bandit Of Mole Hill, E.S. Lampman	*Samuri Of Gold Hill*, Y. Uchida
Patty Reed's Doll, Rachel Laurgaard	*To Touch The Sky*, A. Fink

PROJECT ASSIGNMENTS

Diversity Unit Projects continued...

NAME _____

Project Planning Sheet: Diversity Unit

*My Project is*_____

I need information about _____

_____

_____

My goal is _____

_____

Materials I need are _____

I may need help on _____

_____

_____

Day _____

*Plan*_____

Accomplishment _____

I will judge how well I've done by _____

_____

_____

*I plan to share the results by*_____

APPENDIX A

Social Studies Report (Fifth Grade)
Directions for Oral Reports on a U.S. State

Include the following information in your oral report in the order presented here. Information should be recorded on flash cards and presented to the class at an agreed-upon time. Props and visual aids (photographs, coins, costumes, ect.) may be used, but the oral presentation must be entirely your own (no videos). The report will be equivalent to four test grades, one each in the following subjects: oral language, geography, history, and civics.

1. **Introduce your state and point out on the U.S. map its location.** Identify the surrounding states and bodies of water.

2. **Describe the size of your state** by giving the area in square miles and the greatest distance from north to south and from east to west. Compare the size of your state with California (e.g., California is three times bigger).

3. **Make a large map of your state** showing the major regions (mountains, deserts, plains, etc.), bodies of water, and the location and names of the major cities. Pronounce them, point them out on the map for the class, and describe them. Identify the highest and lowest points of elevation and the capital city. Give the population of the largest city and mention anything else interesting that you may have learned about these places.

4. **Give the population of your state (2000 census).** Include the population density per square mile. Point out on your map where the population is very dense. Explain why people settled in these regions.

5. **Describe the religious** make-up of your state.

6. **Identify the state flower**, the state bird and animal, state tree, and any other symbols that represent your state. Explain how these symbols may have come about, or tell any story that may help the class understand their historical importance.

7. **Make a large flag** of your state and describe the meaning of the colors and symbols.

8. **Describe the government of your state.** Include the name of the governor and the length of the term, the legislature and length of terms, and the number of counties.

9. **Describe the climates in your state** at various times of the year. Include the high and low temperatures and the average yearly precipitation.

10. **What is the state motto**, and what does it mean?

11. **Describe the wildlife in the various regions** of your state (include pictures if you want). Identify any national parks or wildlife preserves.

12. **Describe the economy of your state.** Include the following:

    A. agricultural products
    B. mining (minerals found)
    C. manufacturing (things made in factories)
    D. transportation commonly used
    E. trade (products exported and imported)
    F. businesses (products produced and services that are identified
       with your state)

13. **Describe any cultural traditions** or events you may have learned about. They may relate to music, art, dance, religion, or ethnic events.

The format and content of this project were created and provided by Bruce Dalrymple, 5th Grade Teacher at White Point Elementary School, San Pedro, CA

PROJECT ASSIGNMENTS

14. Make an historical time-line of your state, including major historical events. Use it to point out events while discussing #15.

15. Give a brief history of your state. Include the following information:

    A. How statehood came about.
    B. Most important events and dates in its history.
    C. Most important people in state history and what they accomplished.

16. Identify colleges and universities in your state. Mention areas of study that the college is known for, the nickname, and how that may relate to the culture or history of your state.

17. Imagine you were traveling in your state. Describe for the class three places that you would like to visit and why.

18. Write at least ten questions about your state report to quiz the class. You will give the quiz and correct it.

Do not copy sentences from books. Instead, paraphrase the meaning of what you have read. Try not to read the information to the class. Know your subject well enough so that you can talk to the class instead. You may use your flash cards to remind yourself about what you want to say. Be sure to be a good listener when other students are giving their reports. You are expected to learn from their reports, and you will be quizzed on what they report to the class.

State Projects in Bruce Dalrymple's 5th Grade Classroom, White Point School, San Pedro, CA

APPENDIX A

Egypt Map Project (6th Grade Social Studies)

Due Date: _____

On a piece of 8-1/2 X 11-inch paper, draw a map of Ancient Egypt. Color in all areas of land and bodies of water using colored pencils. Title your map and provide a key.

Show and label all of the following places and features:

–Nile River

–Nile Delta

–First, Second, Third, Fourth, Fifth Cataracts

–Upper Egypt

–Lower Egypt

–Mediterranean Sea

–Red Sea

–Gulf of Suez

–Arabian Desert

–Libyan Desert

–Nubian Desert

–Nubia

–Kush

–Sinai Peninsula

–Cities: Thebes, Memphis, Meroe, Napata, Amarna (also known as Tel El Amarna)

–Project will be graded using the Map Rubric shown on the reverse side of these directions.

Photos by Sierra Weir

Ancient Egypt Maps by Kendall Tardy, Rhiannon Franck-Thompson, and Lynn Chai, 6th Grade Social Studies students of Laura J. Freeman, Dodson Gifted & High Ability Magnet Middle School, San Pedro, CA

PROJECT ASSIGNMENTS

Egypt Map continued...

MAP RUBRIC

5   The map is accurate with the contours of the continent and states detailed: the map is correctly titled and labeled; the coloring is neat, artistic, and shows excellent craftsmanship; there are extra details on the map which go beyond the assigned requirements and indicate much research and time; all requirements are neatly and accurately labeled; the required size art paper is used; the overall impression shows effort and pride.

4   The map is accurate and the contours are detailed; the map is correctly titled and labeled; lots of information is included on the map (theme); the coloring is neat and carefully done; there may be extra details added; the overall impression shows effort and care.

3   The map is generally accurate although some features may not be placed exactly correctly; contours tend to be undetailed but land masses are recognizable; the coloring is adequate but not especially artistic; the map meets the minimal expectations of the assignment; very little information (theme) is demonstrated; overall impression shows some effort.

2   The map may be incorrectly or incompletely labeled; the contours make the map seem distorted; map lacks detailing; the map may not fulfill the minimal requirements; there is little information/research demonstrated on the map; the overall impression is not impressive; the map appears rushed and careless.

1   The map is inaccurate; there is no attempt to color or detail; the map does not fulfill the minimal requirements; the overall impression of the map does not reflect care or effort.

0   Map was not turned in.

The format and content of this project were created and provided by Laura J. Freeman, Dodson Gifted and High Ability Magnet Middle School, RPV, CA

APPENDIX A

African Kingdoms Report

Grading Sheet (Grade 7 Social Studies Report)

*Name*_____

Kingdom of _____

PRESENTATION

Title Page/Heading (10) ____

Table of Contents (10) ____

Picture #1 (5) ____

Picture #2 (5) ____

Map (10) ____

Bibliography (10) ____

Grammar (10) ____

Spelling (10) ____

Overall Presentation (10) ____

Total Score (200) ____

GRADE ____

The format and content of this project were created and provided by Raymond Moser, 7th Grade Social Studies teacher at Dodson Gifted & High Ability Magnet Middle School, San Pedro, CA

CONTENT

Climate and Geography (10) ____

Rise of the Kingdom (10) ____

Agriculture (10) ____

Industry (10) ____

Politics (10) ____

Religion (10) ____

Society (10) ____

Family (10) ____

Arts & Music (10) ____

Biography (10) ____

Fall of Kingdom (10) ____

Legacy of Kingdom ____

Sports & Games (10) ____

Overall Content (10) ____

Content Score (120) ____

PROJECT ASSIGNMENTS

African Kingdoms continued...

African Kingdoms

A Cooperative Research Project

The Kingdom of **Ghana**, The Kingdom of **Mali**, The Kingdom of **Songhai**, The Kingdom of **Kongo**, and The Kingdom of **Zimbabwe** are five major powers over one thousand years of African history and have a lasting influence on Africa's view of itself today. You will be divided into groups of four or five to aid in researching and editing, but you alone will be responsible for the final written product.

Step 1: Research: Each group will gather research materials for citation in the bibliography, including at least three encyclopedias, three books, and three internet sites. You will have at least one day a week to work on the project in class, including the internet and an encyclopedia CD. We will make two visits to the library after the New Year. Besides the groups, the students writing on each kingdom will also meet once during the first week in January to compare the sources they have found. You will submit a preliminary bibliography the first week of school in 2002, Wednesday 9 January. (10 points)

Step 2: Outline: You should begin your outline while you are compiling your bibliography, and should include details on, in order: Climate & Geography; Rise of the Kingdom; Agriculture; Industry; Politics; Religion; Society; Family; Art & Music; Sports & Games; Biography; The Fall of the Kingdom; The Legacy of the Kingdom; or other topics approved by the teacher. This will be due Wednesday 16 January to be examined by your group. The people from each kingdom will meet again to compare outlines. (10 points)

Step 3: Rough Draft: Each of the above sections should be between one-half to one page in length, twelve point font, double spaced, except for the Rise and Fall, which may be longer. It will be due Wednesday 30 January in class for examination by the rest of your group. This will be due in class Friday 25 January. (10 points)

Step 4: Final Draft: The final report will include a title page, table of contents, bibliography, at least one map, and two pictures along with chapters on all the sections listed above and will be due on Friday 1 February. (200 points)

Photos by Sierra Weir

African Masks Created in conjunction with African Kingdom Project by Erica Fitzpatrick (Juno the Bird); Brett Weir (Lord of Fire); and Lonnae Williams (Lion's Mask) of Raymond Moser's 7th Grade Social Studies class

APPENDIX A

African Kingdoms continued...

Sample of Partial Outline for Project

Kongo Kingdom Outline

I. Climate and Geography

A. Climate

1. Kongo is divided into three ecological zones; coastal, middle, and plateau.
2. The coastal section had an average temperature ranging from 25 to 27 degrees Celsius.
3. Rainfall was irregular, and remained at about 400mm.
4. Most extreme conditions occurred near Luanda.
5. The middle section had moderate temperatures without much variation that stayed at about 15-20 degrees.
6. Yearly precipitation averaged over 1,400mm.
7. Third region was plateau.

B. Geography

1. Boundaries going from north clockwise on the compass included the river Kwilu, the river Niari, the Malebo pool, the river Kwango, the river Kwanza, and the Atlantic Ocean.
2. It included parts of what are now Angola and Zaire, and a portion of Congo.
3. The middle ecological zone of Kongo was very hilly, and eventually led to a mountain range.
4. It ran parallel to the coast.

II. Rise of the Kingdom

A. Founded in 1300s (14th Century).

B. First King Nimi a Lukeni married daughter of Kabunga, Kongo chiefand took title of Mani-Kongo.

C. King organized villages into 6 provinces.

D. Powers of Kingdom Mani-Kongo was spiritual and military leader and ruler.

E. Political Influence.

PROJECT ASSIGNMENTS

"Big, Bigger and Bigger"

7th Grade Math Project

This project is due on Thursday, February 7, 2002. Spend quality time working on this at home and in class. In order to get an outstanding grade on the project, you need to turn in all written work, show all calculations, follow all directions, and be mathematically accurate. You may work on the project with one or two other students, but each of you must turn in your own written work.

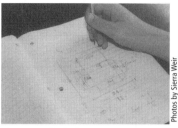
Measure and calculate

1. **Select an object that you would like to enlarge.** Some examples include candy boxes, school supplies, household items, paperback books, and so on. Be creative!

2. **Measure and calculate:** (to the nearest tenth of a cm)
   a. Length in cm
   b. Width in cm
   c. Height in cm
   d. Volume in cubic cm
   e. Surface area in square cm

3. **Your options for enlargement:** Length, width, and height of project can be 3-8 times the length, width, and height of the original object. Be sure to consider how you will get your project to school. Will it fit on the bus? In the car?

Enlarging a Razor Blade Box by Brett Weir

4. **Calculate all NEW measurements** using your enlargement factor BEFORE building the enlarged object.
   a. New length in cm
   b. New width in cm
   c. New height in cm
   d. New volume in cubic cm
   e. New surface area in square cm

5. **Build the enlarged model of your object.** Beware of the following: Your new dimensions must be what you calculated in Step 4. It must be STURDY so it doesn't cave in. The colors must match up as closely as possible and the enlarged object must include relevant artwork.

6. **Written work must include a cover page**, an explanation of how you made your project, measurements and calculations, and a comparison of the original and new volume and surface area.

7. **Written work** – 60 points
   Project – 40 points

8. **ALL WORK SHOULD BE NEAT AND ACCURATE!**

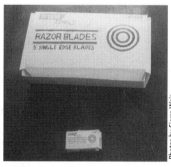
The finished product!

The format and content of this project were created and provided by Joyce Kimura, 7th Grade Math teacher at Dodson Gifted & High Ability Magnet Middle School, RPV, CA

APPENDIX A

Big, Bigger and Bigger continued...

Written Report

Report may be done on the computer (size 12 font) double-spaced. A handwritten report must be written in cursive in blue or black ink.

Cover page must include your name and math class period and the name of the object you enlarged (example: Dove soap) as your title.

Your report of how you made your project should include an explanation of why you chose your object, a list of materials you used, and a time-line explaining the steps you followed.

You may include **drawings, diagrams,** or **photographs**

Measurements and **calculations** must be shown on the worksheet provided by the teacher and must be included in the report.

Include a **summary**. Did you enjoy the project? Why or why not? What difficulties did you encounter? What would you do differently? What could you have done to improve your project? These questions are only suggestions of some of the ideas you could include in your summary. Be original.

BE NEAT AND ACCURATE!!

Enlarged Objects: Rubik's Cube by Victor Kmita; Blue Tip Matches by William McKenna; Trix by Noah Andrade; Juicy Fruit Gum by Sheri Baxter; Kraft Parmesan Cheese by Mercie Maes; and Pocky Biscuits by Haien Yu, Vivian Nguyen, and Stephanie Hanaya

Photos by Sierra Weir

PROJECT ASSIGNMENTS

Norse Mythology

Research Project (Grade 7 English)

You will be writing a four-page research report on a figure in Norse mythology. You will set up your report as follows:

Page One: Three paragraphs

Paragraph One: Name the figure you have been assigned. Explain his or her parentage or creation and provide a physical description.

Paragraph Two: Describe the figure's special abilities and powers. Describe their weaknesses as well.

Paragraph Three: Explain how or if they were worshipped. Describe any holidays or events either named after them or celebrated in their honor. Describe their relationship with other gods and man. Tell about any rivals.

Page Two: Summarize a myth relating to your assigned figure. Three paragraphs

Paragraph One: Briefly summarize relevant information from page one in order to introduce your figure and his or her role in the myth you have selected.

Paragraph Two: Summarize the myth you have chosen. Remember your assigned figures should be an important, if not central, figure in the myth you have selected.

Paragraph Three: Use the above summary to analyze your figure's impact on the Norse world. Was it positive or negative? Was that figure integral or peripheral to Norse culture?

Page Three: Connections – This is your opportunity to connect with the figure assigned. You will be expected to make personal as well as interdisciplinary and cross cultural connections. Three paragraphs

Paragraph One: Explain why you think this deity was important to Norse culture. Be specific and give reasons for your opinions.

Paragraph Two: Cross-cultural and interdisciplinary connections are made here. Do you see any analogous figures in any other mythology or religion you have studied? If so, explain their similarities. If not, explain why you think this figure is unique to Norse mythology.

Paragraph Three: Do you think this figure is, or could be relevant or useful in today's society? Explain your opinion in detail.

The format and content of this project were created and provided by Michele Bethune, 7th Grade English Teacher at Dodson Gifted & High Ability Magnet Middle School, PRV, CA

APPENDIX A

Norse Mythology continued...

Page Four: Works cited.

Preparing the List of Works Cited

Book by a single author:

Pollak, Vivian R. Dickenson: *The Anxiety of Gender Ithaca*: Cornell UP, 1984

Anthology or Compilation:

Seller, Maxine Schwartz, ed. *Ethnic Theater in the United States*.
Westport: Greenwood, 1983

Book by two or more persons:

Janaro, Richard Paul, and Thelma C. Altshuler. *The Art of Being Human*.
2nd ed. New York: Harper, 1983.

A multi-volume work:

Churchill, Winston S. *The Age of Revolution*. New York: Dodd 1957
Vol. 3 of *A History of the English Speaking Peoples*. 4 vols. 1956-58.

An article in a reference book such as an encyclopedia or dictionary:

Unknown author:

"Mandarin." *Encyclopedia Americana*. 1980 ed.

Known Author:

Chippini, Luciano. "Este, House of." *Encyclopedia Britannica*:
Macropaedia. 1974

Article from a monthly periodical

Corcoran, Liz. "Space and the Arts." *Space World* Oct. 1982: 14-17

Article from a newspaper:

Collins, Glenn. "Single-Father Survey Finds Adjustment a Problem."
New York Times 21 Nov. 1983, late ed.: B17

Internet:

Author, I. (Date). Title of article. Name of Periodical [On-line],
xx. Available: Web Address

For further and more in-depth information regarding citations, consult **The MLA Handbook For Writers of Research Papers** (5th Edition), available in libraries and book stores

PROJECT ASSIGNMENTS

Norse Mythology continued...

The mythological figures that were the subject of these reports were ultimately developed into characters for a group project boardgame (see photo). Students were asked to score each group's board game based on the following student-created rubric:

Board Game Score Card for _____

Each of the following is worth 5 points:

Box:

　　Neat_____

　　Sturdy_____

　　Colorful_____

　　Unique_____

Board:

　　Neat_____

　　Colorful_____

　　Connects to Norse Mythology_____

Pieces:

　　Easy to tell apart_____

　　Intact_____

　　Connects to Norse Mythology_____

Rules:

　　Easy to follow_____

　　Fair_____

Playability:

　　Understandable_____

　　Easy to play_____

　　Clear object_____

　　Overall (Worth 10 points each):

　　Spelling, Punctuation, and Grammar
　　Correct_____

Obviously Relates to Norse Mythology_____

Informative_____

Fun_____

**TOTAL
POINTS**_____

Norse Mythology Board Games Created by Ms. Bethune's 7th Grade English Class, Dodson Gifted and High Ability Magnet Middle School, RPV, CA

Photo by Kathie Weir

APPENDIX A

Science Fair Research Report (Middle School)

Sections of the Research Report

Logbook: You will need to get a small spiral notebook that you can use to record everything that you read and do for your science fair project. Your log is written as you go. Include notes, measurements, phone calls, email letters, etc., and be sure to date and time each entry. The logbook will be part of your final project presentation. Remember to have your name on the front cover along with your school and grade.

1. **Title** - The title of your project should be a "catchy," interest-grabbing one that describes your project so that people reading your report can immediately figure out what it is about.

2. **The Problem** - (due November 9, 2001) This is probably the most difficult part of the science fair research project. However, think about what things you're interested in and how you can come up with a question that can be answered through experimentation. Keep in mind that acceptable questions generally begin with "What is the effect of _____ on _____?"

   Some of the terms you could use in the first blank are: temperature, noise, design, density, humidity, wind direction, music, pressure, acid, turbidity, oxygen, etc. Some terms you could use in the second blank are: seed germination, rusting, growth, rotting, ripening, wave frequency, surface hardness, learning, fatigue. Remember, if you are planning to conduct an experiment on plants, you will need to grow them in a greenhouse or indoor environment during the winter. Please do not conduct any experiment that is unsafe or may cause pain or harm to any animal.

3. **Background Research** – This is the section where you will utilize all your research skills to find information related to your topic. Remember, the main objective in requiring students to participate in a science fair is to develop research skills and critical thinking! This research report will be turned in two parts. Let's say, for example, that you have decided to conduct an experiment on, "The Effect of Water Termperature on the Breathing Rate of Goldfish." Part I of your research report (due November 30, 2001) would include the following information:

   I. A brief explanation (one-half a page) of your general science field of study (i.e., zoology, anatomy, physiology, etc.)

   II. Information on the general characteristics of goldfish and related species, including the anatomy and physiology of your particular species of golfish, the behavior and habitat, as well as the conditions under which goldfish live.

   III. Information about respiration or breathing in fish, the effect of water temperature on the behavior of fish, the anatomy and physiology of gills, and the gaseous exchange of oxygen and carbon dioxide.

   IV. Remember, you must keep records of all your sources of information and list them in a bibliography (including websites!). I will give you a handout for the proper way to do this. Part II of your research report (due January 18, 2002) requires you to do a more in-depth study. Simply relying on encyclopedias, reference books, textbooks, etc., is not enough. Now, you will need to access information from science periodicals (magazines, journals, etc.), internet websites that are related to your specific question (Temperature and Respiration Rates in Goldfish). This may require hours of searching for the right information. You will come to dead-ends along the way. However, when you finally find the source that has the information you so desperately need, it is very rewarding to find it!

The format and content of this project were created and provided by Alan Kusumoto, 7th Grade Science Teacher, Dodson Gifted and High Ability Magnet Middle School, RPV, CA

PROJECT ASSIGNMENTS

Science Fair continued...

For your experiment on the effect of temperature on the breathing rate of goldfish, you will need to find information on:

I. Experiments similar to yours (how temperature affects breathing in all animals)

II. Other experiments on goldfish

III. Experiments just like yours and the results they came up with.

IV. The advice of experts (veterinarian, fish store personnel, college science professors, high school biology teachers, etc.)

4. Hypothesis - (due December 7, 2001) This is a prediction of what the results will be before you perform the experiment. You may begin the hypothesis with the following statement:

"I think that if I_____, then it will result in _____.

5. Materials/Procedures – (due December 7, 2001). Once you have decided on a question, you need to figure out what materials you need and what procedures you will follow to conduct the experiment. Keep in mind that you will need to have (in most cases) a control and a variable group(s). All experiment conditions need to be kept the same (constant) except for the variable you are testing.

Example: In the experiment on water temperature and breathing in goldfish, the following factors should be the same: the size and age of the goldfish; the size and type of the fishbowl or aquarium; water quality; lighting; time of day that measurements are made; the amount of time the fish are observed; etc. Make a step-by-step list of what you will do to answer your experiment question. Be as detailed as possible, so that someone else can repeat your procedures and come up with the same result. Otherwise, the credibility of your results could be challenged because of an oversight or error on your part!

6. Data – (due February 8, 2002) The results of your experiment should be recorded carefully. Data can be measured in different ways. Preferably, you will have numbers or percentages that you can measure and compare by using charts, tables, and graphs. You will be taught how to use spreadsheets (Microsoft Excel) to create these. This is a required component and needs to be done on a computer.

7. Conclusions – (due February 15, 2002) Using your data and observations, try to answer your original question. Is your hypothesis correct? Summarize what happened in your experiment.

8. Evaluations and Recommendations for Further Research – (due February 15, 2002) Summarize any difficulties or problems you had doing the experiment. What could you have done differently? Did you need to change the procedure and repeat your experiment?

9. Display Board Design – (due March 1) Drawing of planned design of display board.

10. Turn In Your Project to Carter Hall: - (due March 8, 2002). Set up project in designated area in the morning between 7:30 – 8:00 a.m.

11. Take Home Project – March 16, 2002

Science Fair Notebook #1

1. Title Page:

By,
Your Name
Class
School
Date

(Center all information on this page)

2. Table of Contents:

Page #
Problem
Background Research
Interview
Bibliography

(Be sure to number each page and include page numbers)

3. Investigative Question

(What do you want to find out?)

4. Background Research Part I

(General information about your field of study, experiment, and interview)

5. Background Research Part II

(Specific information about your experiment and related experiments, similar to yours – Compare data and results.)

6. Bibliography

(List all books, magazines, and other sources of information. You must use the proper bibliographic form!)

APPENDIX A

Science Fair continued...

Science Fair Notebook #2

1. Title Page:

> (Same information as Notebook #1)

2. Table of Contents:

> Page #
> Abstract
> Hypothesis
> Materials
> Procedure
> Data/Observations
> Graphs/Charts/Photos
> Results
> Conclusions
> Recommendations for Future Research
> Bibliography
> Acknowledgements

3. Abstract:

> (One-page explanation of what you are attempting to do and why you're doing it)

4. Hypothesis:

> (Your answer to your question before you conduct the experiment.)

5. Materials:

> (A list of all the materials you used in your experiment)

6. Procedures:

> (List the steps that you followed in doing your experiment. Make sure they are clearly written, so that I or someone else can perform your experiment and get similar results.)

Trajectories, by Brett Weir and
Psychic Abilities by Sierra Weir

Photo by Kathie Weir

7. Data/Observations:

> (This is all the information gathered while performing the experiment.)

8. Graphs and Charts:

> (Use Excel or Power Point or a similar program Record measurements in metric system (cm, mm, degrees, celcius, etc).)

9. Results/Conclusions:

> (Summarize your findings from your experiment data. Your conclusion should be based on the results you found in your experiment. Be sure to compare your conclusion to your hypothesis.)

10. Future Research:

> (Any ideas that you may have thought of during your experiment. You may actually do further experimenting later.)

11. Bibliography:

12. Acknowledgements:

> (Credit anyone who helped you and explain what he or she did. Be sure to include the expert you interviewed.)

Example:

1. All measurements: Size, shape, height, width, distances, weight, temperatures, before and after the experiment.
2. Pictures/Drawings: Before, during, and after experiment
3. Time measurements
4. Changes in behavior
5. Observe the CONTROL: Write down what happened to the group that had no experimenting performed on it.
6. Changes in temperature
7. Counting: (number of leaves, etc.)
8. Degrees of brightness, color, etc.
9. Record unexpected results

PROJECT ASSIGNMENTS

Eighth Grade English Book Report

Book Report #2 – Characterization

Introduction: At the heart of most great stories are intriguing characters. It doesn't matter if they're heroes or villains, males or females, young or old, mortal beings or supernatural creatures. It's the writer's job to make sure they grab the reader's attention and don't let go. A writer creates such powerful personalities by a process called characterization, which involves much more than simply describing what a character looks like or what he or she is wearing.

For this book report, I'd like to introduce you to a device called a Character Wheel. Each of the six spokes on the wheel represents a method of characterization. To better understand how the wheel works, take a look at the sample wheel... now: travel back in time to London during the mid-1800s. Inside the laboratory of Dr. Henry Jekyll, a strange experiment has been underway for months. Now a gruesome murder has been committed. The prime suspect is a mysterious midnight prowler known as Mr. Hyde. These two characters are at the heart of Robert Louis Stevenson's classic novel of good and evil, *Dr. Jekyll and Mr. Hyde*. As you look at the wheel, you will see how Stevenson has used each spoke of the wheel to create his hero.

ALL THE DETAILS:

The Basics: In this book report, you will focus on characterization. You will create character wheels for two of the major characters in your book and you will analyze the heroic qualities of one of these characters. You will also analyze and evaluate just how successful the author was in creating believable, three-dimensional characters.

The Requirements: (Use this as your checklist)

Book Information – include an illustration/design related to your book, title (underlined or italics), author, publisher, date first published, your name, date, and period.

Vocabulary – research and define the following terms. Include on your project (See *Elements of Literature, Handbook of Literary Terms and Techniques*, pages 705 – 718 and last page of packet.):

Character	Antagonist	Minor Character
Flat Character	Dynamic Character	Indirect Characterization
Main Character/Progagonist	Hero/Heroine	Round Character
Static Character	Characterization	Direct Characterization

Character Wheels for two major characters – A character wheel is an ingenious device that has 6 spokes. Each spoke on the wheel represents one of six methods of characterization used by writers to create intriguing characters with powerful personalities. For each character you are analyzing, find and analyze passages from your book that show the author using each spoke. Draw a character wheel with six spokes, label each spoke and add excerpts from the novel that show the author's use of each method (be sure to use quotation marks and cite the page number).

Spoke #1 – Physical Description: How has the author described the character's appearance? Has the author appealed to one or more of the 5 senses?

Spoke #2 – Setting: Physical details about a character do not often reveal important background information about that character, but where a preson lives or spends time can reveal a great deal.

Spoke #3 – Behavior Traits and Personality: What vivid verbs has the author chosen to push the character into action and bring him/her to life?

Spoke #4 – Thoughts and Motivation: Has the author let you see into the mind of the character to reveal what he fears, desires, regrets, loves, or wants?

Spoke #5 – Speech: Speech is not only what a character says, but also how he or she says it. Look at the character's dialogue and/or dialect.

Spoke #6 – Reaction of Others/Relationships with Others: This allows the reader to see the character through the eyes of another character. The way people react to a character reveals information about that character.

The format and content of this project were created and provided by Linda Velasco, 8th Grade English Teacher, Dodson Gifted & High Ability Magnet Middle School, RPV, CA

APPENDIX A

Book Report continued...

Analysis of Heroic Qualities: Is the Main Character a Hero?

In literature, a heroic character is often an extraordinarily courageous individual who performs selfless deeds or makes personal sacrifices. However, as we have seen so recently, an ordinary person who faces difficult challenges can also be a hero.

In the book you just read, would you say that the main character is a hero? What qualities of a hero does this individual possess? In one well-organized paragraph (topic sentence, supporting details, concluding sentence) – see Write Source 2000, #425, the one-paragraph essay answer), explain why you believe that this character is or is not a hero, using the information on your character wheel and other details from the story to support your point of view.

Use the new vocabulary, compound and complex sentences (see *Fifteen Steps to Better Writing*, steps 8 and 9), and strong nouns, verbs, adjectives, and adverbs. As always, check your work carefully to find and correct any Grammar Crimes and/or Often Overlooked Proofreading Slipups (OOPS!!).

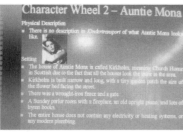
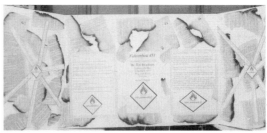

Two Character Wheel Projects: **Kindertransport** (by Olga Levy Drucker), Project by Nic Jordan; and **Fahrenheit 451** (by Ray Bradbury), Project by Kevin Hagaman. Both students of Linda Velasco's 8th Grade English class at Dodson Gifted & High Ability Magnet Middle School, RPV, CA

Analysis/Evaluation of Characterization: Has the Author Created a Believable Character?

How successful has your author been in creating believable, three-dimensional characters that are well-rounded and dynamic? In one well-organized paragraph (topic sentence, supporting details, concluding sentence), discuss which character you found to be the most interesting and believable in your book. What kind of relationship would you have with this character if he or she were real? Use at least three details from the character wheel to support your answer.

Presentation:

You may present this assignment as a freestanding flat or tri-fold display, a creatively-shaped book, or a Power Point presentation. Your project must show good craftsmanship, creativity, and attention to detail, and your ability to follow directions. Use your imagination and enjoy the project!

Due Date: Your book report will be due on: _____

Please fill out the following information and include this label on your final product:

My book's title is: _____

Author: _____

Publisher: _____

Date first published: _____

We have read and understand the requirements for Book Report #2: _____

Name: _____

Parent Signature _____

PROJECT ASSIGNMENTS

The Umbrella Mobile (Eighth Grade Social Studies)

The Different Levels and Branches of our Federal System

1. You need to cut out 5 "umbrellas" of decreasing sizes. Each one represents a different level of government in our federal system.

2. Each umbrella needs 2 to 3 lines/areas reserved at the top for labeling the level of government. Each umbrella also has to be divided so as to represent the different powers/branches of government. To do this, label the bottom three sections (arches) **Legislative**, **Executive**, and **Judicial**.

3. Label each umbrella as follows, starting with the largest:

    A. Label the highest level (largest) **national government**. Write our **nation's name** near the top. Under our nation, write the location of the **capital**.

    B. Label the 2nd largest: state. Write your **state's name** near the top. Under the state, write the location of the **capital**.

    C. Label the 3rd **county**. Write your **county's name**.

    D. The 4th is for the **city** you live in. (Remember: San Pedro, Wilmington, Harbor City are regions within the City of Los Angeles.)

    E. The fifth is for a district such as LAUSD, MTA, Water District, Library District, etc. Some rural areas might even have a Mosquito Abatement District.

4. To fill out the **branches of government** you may have to use a variety of resources such as a text book, almanac, encyclopedia, internet, and the **government pages of your telephone book**.

    A. On the **FRONT** of each umbrella you will need to **fill out**:

        a. The name/title of the Chief Executive in the **Executive** section.

        b. The names/titles of the Legislators in the **Legislative** section.

        c. The names/titles of the Judiciary in the **Judicial** section.

    B. On the **BACK** of each umbrella **write down** at least 10 duties, agencies and offices (and/or situations) that each level of government is responsible for.

The format and content of this project were created and provided by Teresa L. Baumann, 8th Grade Social Studies teacher at Dodson Gifted & High Ability Magnet Middle School, RPV, CA

Umbrella Mobile Project

Photo by Kathie Weir

APPENDIX B

Stuff You Can Make at Home

Paper Maché Mask Recipe

By the way, the term, "paper maché" comes from a French phrase, "papier maché," which means "mashed paper."

First, Make Paper Maché

Ingredients (for one mask)

1/2 Cup of white flour

2 Cups cold water

2 Cups boiling water

3 Tablespoons of sugar

1. Combine flour and the cold water in a bowl. My grandmother swore that sifting the flour first made a better paste. Try it both ways.
2. Boil two cups of water in a sauce pan (Parental supervision required)
3. Add the cold flour-water mixture to the boiling water.
4. Bring mixture to a boil again.
5. Remove from heat and stir in sugar.
6. Allow mixture to cool.
7. As it cools, it will thicken and be ready to use.

Balloon Mask

Materials

1. A round balloon
2. Lots of newspaper
3. Paper Mache paste
4. Aluminum foil
5. Yarn
6. Cotton balls
7. Masking tape

Directions

1. Spread newspaper, plastic, or tarps over all work surfaces.
2. Blow up balloon and tie it closed.
3. Set balloon on a disposable plastic container (e.g., margarine or cream cheese)
   If you use a cup or bowl, cover it with plastic to avoid cleanup.
4. Tear several newspaper pages into strips that are about one inch wide by 8-10 inches long.

5. Dip your newspaper strips into your pan of paper maché paste, then spread them onto the balloon. Continue until your entire balloon is covered, excluding the area where the balloon is resting on the container and any openings desired for eyes, or mouth. Let the first layer dry before continuing.

Mask and photo by Sierra Weir

Paper Maché Mask

6. After the first layer dries, you can use various materials such as cardboard, tape, aluminum foil, cotton balls, fabric, or yarn to build up facial features. For example, you can make a nose with a piece of egg carton. Masking tape is recommended to hold things in place.
7. You should continue to layer paper mache onto your balloon. Two or three more layers are advised, with complete drying in between.
8. When the mask is completely dry, pop the balloon and remove it through the bottom opening. Carefully cut the back half of the model away, leaving only the front half as your mask.
9. Paint or decorate your mask as desired, with glitter, ribbons, etc.
10. Paste yarn, string, or colored cotton on for hair.

Play Dough

2 cups of white flour
1 cup of salt
4 tablespoons of cream of tartar
2 cup ice water
4 teaspoons of food coloring

Mix the flour, salt and cream of tartar with water in a saucepan over high to medium-high heat. Add food coloring. Stir till boiling 3-5 minutes, being careful not to scorch. Remove from heat. Let cool. Store in sealed plastic ware.

The main problem with make-it-yourself play dough is that it is difficult to achieve the same bright colors as what your kids are used to. Otherwise, this recipe will produce lots of play dough at a fairly low cost. If you keep it in the fridge, it lasts a long time, too. Keep it on hand and your kids can use it to fashion models or figures for elementary school projects.

STUFF YOU CAN MAKE AT HOME

Making a Pop-Up Book

Materials:

One sheet of 9 x 12-inch Construction paper, any color

2-3 Sheets of 8.5 x 11-inch white paper (more if you are writing a longer book)

Shapes or scenes colored and cut out for pop-up pieces

Crayons or Markers

Glue

One very good idea

Instructions:

1. Fold the construction paper in half to make your book cover.
2. Write the title and author's name on the front.
3. Illustrate the cover and color with crayons or markers.
4. Decide which scenes or characters will pop up.
5. Draw those characters and scenes and cut them out.
6. Fold a sheet of white paper in half. Put the fold at the top, then open.
7. On the top half, draw your background for the pop-up.
8. On the lower half, write your story.
9. Cut two evenly spaced tabs out of the fold, then push them forward into your book. These will form a right angle square on which to glue your scenes.
10. Glue scenes or characters to the tabs.
11. Each pop-up scene is a separate construction. Make as many as you like, then put them in order.
12. Glue the pages together in order (fronts to backs of pop-up units).
13. Glue the back of the first page to the front cover and the back of the last page to the back cover.
14. Be sure to sign and date your one-of-a-kind pop-up book.

Book and Photo by Sierra Weir

Pop-Up Book

APPENDIX C

Glossary

Abstract – a short summary of a document or research paper, placed at the beginning of the paper to identify its subject matter and scope.

Bibliography – a list of the books, films, magazine articles, websites, and other sources of information that a student has reviewed and relied on in preparing a research paper or project. See example in the Norse Mythology Report, Appendix A.

Book Report – a paper that summarizes, critiques, and/or evaluates a book that a student has read.

Classroom Helper – a parent who volunteers to help out in the classroom. You must fill out the appropriate paperwork and arrange a schedule with the teacher. Not to be confused with "classroom aide," which is a paid position.

Collage – an artistic composition consisting of or including flat materials, such as newspaper, photographs, cloth, etc., pasted on a picture surface. Teachers often assign students to create a collage based on a certain theme or topic, in order to enhance their learning in that area.

Communication – the act of transmitting or exchanging ideas or information through the methods of speech or writing.

Conclusion – the last section of a paper, in which the writer explains his final opinion, based on the topics or ideas he discussed in the main part of his paper.

Cooperation – the act of working together toward a common end; joint action.

Coordination – the condition of working with others in a harmonious, integrated, and effective manner to achieve a goal.

Creative – having the power or ability to create; characterized by originality of thought and execution.

Critique – the act of giving one's opinion about the work or performance of another, which is always more effective if done in a friendly and supportive manner.

Deadline – the date on which a paper or project must be finished and handed in.

Design – to sketch, plan, and create with skill, as a work of art. To decide ahead of time how something will look, then construct it accordingly, being mindful of size, shape, color, texture, and setting.

Diorama – an exhibit consisting of modeled figures or objects, etc., set in a naturalistic foreground w/ a painted background. For school projects, dioramas are often created in shoeboxes, wine boxes, or other small boxes set on their sides, with the open end acting as a type of staging area.

Demonstration – an exhibition and explanation of a subject, theory, or process by means of examples, experiments, displays, etc.

Essay – a short composition dealing with a single topic and typically personal in approach.

Field Trip – a school-sponsored trip that can last from a few hours to the entire school day, which gives children in one or more classrooms an opportunity to visit area attractions, including museums, nature centers, theater performances, and other interesting sites. Parent volunteers are usually required as chaperones.

Fundraiser – an organized sale of a particular product or products during a specified time period, for the purpose of raising money for a non-profit organization.

Group Project – a project assigned to a group of two or more students, who are required to jointly create and execute it for a collective or semi-collective grade. Teachers generally grant long deadlines on group projects, sometimes giving as much as two or three months' notice. Group projects may be conducted entirely in school, entirely outside of school, or half and half.

GLOSSARY

Homophone – a word that sounds like another word, but is spelled differently and has a different meaning, e.g., wood and would; paws and pause; reed and read.

Hypothesis – an unproved scientific conclusion drawn from known facts and used as a basis for further investigation and experimentation; the starting point for all science projects.

Illustrate – to decorate with drawings, photographs, magazine pictures, or the like.

Individual Project – a project assigned to each child individually to create and execute on his own (or with help from parents). Individual projects can be long-term or short-term in scope, depending on their complexity.

Introduction – a section at the beginning of a paper, which introduces the topic to be presented, as well as the author's reasons for presenting it.

Methodology – an explanation of the methods that the author used to undertake the research or experimentation that is the subject of his or her writing.

Model – an object, usually in miniature and often built according to scale, that represents something to be made or something already existing.

Paraphrase – to restate something in one's own words.

Plagiarize – to copy the work of another person (e.g., another student, a teacher, or an author) and pass it off as your own work.

Presentation – generally a short assignment, where your child is required to give a 3-5 minute talk about a subject or demonstrate to the class his expertise in doing something, e.g., "How to tie nautical knots" or "How to make sushi."

Project – any activity or set of activities, academic or otherwise, that requires planning, research, creativity, energy, and sustained interest to complete. Projects can include assignments your child gets from the teacher, but can also describe a parent volunteer's ongoing commitment to some aspect of the school's overall success, e.g., fundraising efforts, classroom assistance, arranging and chaperoning field trips, serving on parent-teacher committees and boards, etc.

Research Report – a formal academic paper that includes an abstract, introduction, methodology, table of contents, body, and conclusion. It is usually several pages long and either deals with one or more in-depth topics (e.g., analyzing or comparing literature) or reports on scientific experimentation or surveys. Beginning in the fifth and sixth grades, your child will be assigned to write progressively more detailed and original research reports.

School Spirit – a feeling of ardent loyalty and devotion to one's school, often manifested by wearing school colors, singing school songs, and supporting school sports and academic teams.

Scientific Method – a specific step-by-step method of conducting scientific experiments which allows the experimenter to obtain valid results. Beginning in Kindergarten, students learn to prepare their science projects based on the scientific method.

Summary – a concise or condensed version of a longer work, which explains the main points or theme of the longer work.

Volunteer – one who enters into any service of his own free will.

Workroom Assistant – a volunteer who helps out teachers by performing cutting, labeling, laminating, and other chores in the school workroom.

INDEX

INDEX

INDEX

INDEX

INDEX

INDEX

about the author

Kathie Weir

Photo by Christina Adams

Kathie Weir, mother of a 12-year-old (Brett) and 15-year-old (Sierra), has spent the last nine years coaching her children through increasingly complex school projects, papers, and presentations. She has served as a PTO board member, helped out in the classroom, and coordinated scores of fundraisers and extra-curricular activities. Her experience as an active volunteer parent and substitute teacher has brought her into contact with dozens of dedicated public school teachers, many of whom contributed project assignments as well as their insight. Kathie holds an MFA degree in Fiction Writing, and is also the author of *A Parent's Guide to Los Angeles.* She has published numerous articles and essays about children and child rearing.

Photo by Kathie Weir

Brett Weir, after finishing the 2002 L.A. Marathon

Photo by Kathie Weir

Sierra Weir, hunting for interesting rocks at the beach.

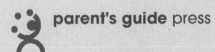

parent's guide press

Good For You.
Good For Your Kids.

The only book about kids and the Internet to be published in the last two years.

"(An) imaginative, valuable resource"

—American Library Association

A Parent's Guide to THE INTERNET
ISBN 0-9675127-9-4
$19.95 (December 2001)

208 Pages —Trade Paperback—**Available in Library Bindings**
Hundreds of Website Listings, Dozens of Illustrations, Index

• **The project oriented non-technical guide to family Internet use.** Dozens of hands-on projects for parents and children help de-mystify the Internet and lay bare issues of privacy, youth-targeted marketing, and safety.

• **Written by Ilene Raymond**, an award winning writer and essayist who has taught at Temple University and Pennsylvania State University. Her articles and fiction have appeared in numerous national publications, including Good Housekeeping, Redbook, Cosmopolitan, Readers Digest, Ladies House Journal, and Mademoiselle. She lives outside Philadelphia with her husband and two sons.

• **HTML explained.** How building a family Web site helps parents and children better understand the Internet (and have fun at the same time).

• **A brief history of the Internet** (and why the Internet is more than the World Wide Web and vice versa).

• **E-mail, Discussion Groups, FTP, IRC Chat:** the Internet that isn't the Web and the opportunities for enlightenment— and abuse— they offer.

• **Advice from experts** such as Slashdot columnist Jon Katz, MaMaMedia.com founder Idit Harel, researcher Michael Antecol and many others: Internet developers, child psychology experts, homeschooling parents, academics, and involved educators. All share insights on how best to use the Internet in the home. In short: Parents need to be involved with their children's Internet activity. The Internet is not a teacher, parent, sibling, babysitter or friend, though it is a powerful communication medium that can help children, grow, learn, meet, and explore.

• **Scores of Web sites** to explore and enjoy, from games to filtering services, online encyclopedias to blogs.

• **A concise glossary** of common Internet and computer terms makes the jargon comprehensible.

• **Indexed** for easy reference.

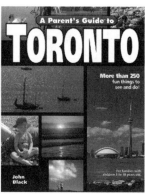